TEACH YOURSELF BOOKS

SEAMANSHIP

Seamanship – the professional skill of the seaman – is the art of handling ships in an efficient and expert manner. This book presents the basic aspects of good seamanship clearly and concisely, and is mainly concerned to cover the Board of Trade's requirements for Efficient Deck Hands. However, it is hoped that the contents will prove as useful to the layman interested in understanding the rudiments of seamanship as to the young seaman learning his trade.

This book sets out to be a presentation of the basic aspects of the art of seamanship, and the author has presented his facts in an admirable manner.

... This is a very nice little book, one from which any young gentlemen going to sea would profit.

The Marine Observer

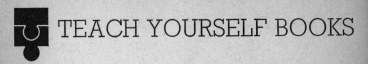 TEACH YOURSELF BOOKS

SEAMANSHIP

T. F. Wickham

*Formerly Seamanship Instructor
at the National Nautical School
Portishead, Somerset*

Revised by

N. Hefford

*Deputy Headmaster,
the National Nautical School,
Portishead, Somerset*

ST. PAUL'S HOUSE   WARWICK LANE   LONDON EC4P 4AH

First printed 1954
Second edition 1972
Second impression 1973

ISBN 0 340 12494 6

Printed in Great Britain for The English Universities Press, Ltd, by C. Tinling & Co. Ltd, London and Prescot.

FOREWORD

Seamanship is a subject for enthusiasts and enthusiasm for it comes from a love of the sea and of ships. It is sincerely hoped that this presentation of the basic aspects of the art of good seamanship will assist all who wish to learn and practise it. No previous knowledge of the subject has been presupposed and the work is mainly concerned to cover the Board of Trade's requirements for Efficient Deck Hands and First Year Apprentices. Thus it is really a manual of *facts* designed to instruct the uninitiated and to help its readers towards becoming able and competent seamen.

The author wishes to record his indebtedness and pay tribute to the training vessel *St. Briavels* of the South American Saint Line, and to her Master, Captain A. A. Havers, R.N., Retd., under whose command it was his privilege to serve.

T. F. WICKHAM

Note to the 1972 Edition

Seamanship – the professional skill of the seaman – remains basically the same. It is the art of handling ships and their equipment in an efficient and expert manner. Modern ships with their intricate and complex equipment, however, call for more skills and knowledge on the part of the seaman than ever before.

This book has been revised with this in mind, so that the young seaman learning his trade, as well as the interested layman, can acquire an up-to-date knowledge of the modern trends in ships, navigation and communication data.

Thus, apart from the new Rules regarding the Prevention of Collisions at Sea, and the new Signal Code and Distress Signals, the chapters revised are those mainly concerned where new equipment has been introduced, i.e. the increasing use of synthetic ropes; the acceptance of inflatable liferafts and ancillary gear; the mechanical cargo hatch covers and modern methods of handling cargo. Because of the ever increasing size of the modern tanker and its complex systems, this section has been dealt with at some length.

The book is still compiled for the beginner who wishes to learn the rudiments of seamanship; also for those seeking information relating to everyday seamanship problems, and for the young seaman who is preparing for advancement.

The revised regulations and requirements relating

to examinations for advancement have been included to enable the reader to appreciate the practical value of the information in the pages of this book.

N. HEFFORD

CONTENTS

ACKNOWLEDGMENTS

The author and publishers wish to acknowledge with thanks the permission of the Controller of H.M. Stationery Office to reproduce in this book the following Crown Copyright material:

(a) Extracts from Board of Trade Notice No. M.580 – Issue of A.B. and Efficient Deck Hand Certificates.
(b) Signals of the Life-saving Services (Board of Trade Rescue Signal Table).
(c) Boat Landing Signals.
(d) The International Regulations for the Prevention of Collisions at Sea (in force 1st September, 1965).

They also wish to express their thanks to RFD–GQ Ltd., who kindly provided material for use in the section on Inflatable Liferafts.

CHAPTER 1

SHIP ROUTINE AND SHIPS

The Crew

The crew of any ship, from the small coaster with a complement of fifteen or twenty men to the largest liner with a complement approaching two thousand, is formed from a similar pattern. A ship's company is divided into three departments, each having its own particular duties to perform and yet each being very closely connected with the other, working in union and harmony to form, on the ideal ship, a perfect team and a complete unit. The supreme head of this unit is, of course, the ship's Master or Captain.

The Engine Department

This department, as the name implies, is concerned with the smooth running of the ship's main engines, which is the source of power which turns the propeller, thus driving the ship through the water. On a steamship this department is also responsible for many smaller auxiliary engines, such as pumps for providing water to hoses for washing down decks, water to fire hoses, and water supply in cabins and bathrooms, etc. There are also suction pumps for removing water from various compartments and feed pumps for ensuring an even water level in boilers. The auxiliary engines also include a condenser which turns the used steam from the engines back into water. This water is then passed through a filter, re-heated and passed back to the boilers. There are evaporators which turn salt water to fresh by boiling it and collecting the steam, dynamos to produce electricity for lighting and power, and sometimes refrigerating machinery for cooling cargo and provisions. At the back (stern) of the ship is another auxiliary called the steering engine which is used for turning the rudder (see Fig. 2a, page 28) and on the main deck of the ship are a number of winches which are used for the loading or discharging of a ship's cargo.

Controlling this very important section of the ship is the Chief Engineer and under him are his assistant officers, the second, third, fourth and fifth engineers. This would be the case on the average merchantman of, say, 8000 tons gross, but on smaller ships the number of assistants would be comparatively less and on larger vessels proportionately more. On ships carrying chilled or frozen cargoes there are also several refrigerating engineers, who are responsible to the Chief Engineer but are concerned solely with the efficient running of the refrigerating plant. Below the engineer officers are men known as Donkeymen Greasers, whose job it is to assist the officers, oil the engines and act as foremen or supervisors to men known as Firemen Trimmers. The latter are the men who actually fire the boilers and maintain the pressure of steam necessary to turn the engines.

The Catering Department
This department is divided into two sections:
1. The galley staff, which is concerned with the preparation of food and is presided over by the Ship's Cook or Chef.

2. Those concerned with the ship's accounts, the general cleanliness of the interior and the serving of food, which is administered by a Purser.

The number of assistants to the Ship's Cook depends upon the size of the ship. The average number is two or three, but this number would be comparatively greater in the case of a large passenger ship.

The Purser of a passenger liner is a very important member of the crew. He must be essentially intelligent and diplomatic, and needs, at times, a keen sense of humour. His job includes the ship's business accounts, wages, the ordering of stores and provisions, disputes, complaints and queries of passengers and crew, and, in fact, almost any question concerned with administration. Responsible to the Purser on such a vessel is the Chief Steward, who controls a number of stewards, pantry boys and cabin boys who are engaged to wait on tables, clean out cabins and passageways, and contribute generally to the comfort of passengers and crew.

The ordinary freighter or tanker does not carry a Purser—the Chief Steward being responsible to the Master for all the stores, catering, etc.

The Deck Department

This is the executive department which is responsible for the navigating, manoeuvring and safe handling of the ship, for all signals made between ship and shore, for the handling and delivery of cargo, for the general maintenance of the ship, and for the control and operation of all life-saving devices.

The head of this department is the Chief Officer,

who is assisted by second, third and sometimes fourth officers. The able seamen, ordinary seamen and deck boys are supervised in their work by a man known as the Boatswain (pronounced Bosn), the latter being responsible to the deck officers. A Ship's Carpenter is also carried who rates the same as a Boatswain and is responsible to the deck officers for work done. At least one Radio Officer is carried on all deep sea vessels who is responsible for all ship-to-ship and ship-to-shore communications.

A boy going to sea in the deck department would start his career as a deck boy, rising by merit to a Junior Ordinary Seaman (J.O.S.), and thence by merit and length of service to Senior Ordinary Seaman (S.O.S.); after a minimum sea service of 1 year, and if over the age of 18 years, he can qualify by examination for an Efficient Deck Hand (E.D.H.). Finally, after a minimum of $2\frac{1}{2}$–3 years' sea service, depending on time spent in pre-sea training, he can obtain his Able Bodied Seaman's Certificate of Competency. This Certificate is issued by a Superintendent of a Mercantile Marine Office only when a seaman provides proof of the following requirements:

  (a) Passed the qualifying examination for E.D.H.
  (b) Obtained the age of 18 years.
  (c) Performed the appropriate sea service.
  (d) Holds a steering certificate.
  (e) In possession of a Lifeboatman's Certificate.

General Purpose Rating

Until quite recently, a deck hand over the age of 18, in possession of a steering ticket and with 1 year's sea service could apply for the E.D.H. qualifying examination. However, the regulations were revised in 1970 to make provision for a new rating, then recently introduced and known as a General Purpose (G.P.) rating. The G.P. rating is an 'all-rounder' who is sufficiently skilled to perform tasks anywhere in the ship, i.e. deck, engine-room and occasionally catering. Some shipping companies, mostly operating tankers, have certain selected ships manned by G.P. ratings and carry out their own training and conversion.

G.P. ratings are eligible to apply for the E.D.H. qualifying examination after 18 months reckonable sea-service, or between 12 and 18 months if they have served partly in a deck (or engine room) rating and partly in a G.P. rating, the periods counting proportionately.

Qualifying Examination
The qualifying examination for E.D.H. is oral and practical only, and is conducted by Board of Trade Nautical Surveyors at most large British ports. Board of Trade Notice M.580 states that the examination shall be based on the following syllabus:

Nautical Knowledge:
1. The meaning of common nautical terms.
2. The names and functions of various parts of a ship—for example, decks, compartments, ballast tanks, bilges, air pipes, strum boxes.
3. Knowledge of the compass card 0° to 360°. Ability to report the approximate bearing of an object in degrees or points on the bow.
4. Reading, streaming and handling a patent log.

5.   Markings on a hand line, taking a cast of the hand lead and correctly reporting the sounding obtained.

6.   Marking of the anchor cable.

7.   Understanding helm orders.

8.   The use of life-saving and fire-fighting appliances.

Practical Work (tested as far as possible by practical demonstration):

9.   Knots, hitches and bends in common use:

Reef knot	Bowline and bowline on the bight
Timber hitch	Sheet bend, double and single
Clovehitch	Sheepshank
Rolling hitch	Round turn and two half hitches
Figure of eight	Marlinspike hitch
Wall and crown	

To whip a rope's end using plain or palm and needle whipping.

To put a seizing on rope and wire. To put a stopper on a rope or wire hawser, and derrick lift.

10.   Splicing plaited and multi-strand manilla and synthetic fibre rope, eye splice, short splice and back splice. Splicing wire rope, eye splicing using a locking tuck. Care in use of rope and wire.

11.   Slinging a stage, rigging a bosn's chair and pilot ladder.

12.   Rigging a derrick. Driving a winch; general precautions to be taken before and during the

operation of a winch whether used for working cargo or for warping.

13. The use and operation of a windlass in anchor work and in warping. Safe handling of moorings with particular reference to synthetic-fibre ropes and self-tensioning winches.

Precautions to be taken in the stowage of chain cable and securing the anchors for sea.

14. A knowledge of the gear used in cargo work and an understanding of its uses. General maintenance with particular reference to wires, blocks and shackles.

15. The safe handling of hatch covers, including mechanical hatch covers, battening down and securing hatches and tank lids.

16. If no Lifeboatman's Certificate is held, a candidate will be required to satisfy the examiner that:

    (a) He understands the general principles of boat management and can carry out orders relating to lifeboat launching and operation, and the handling of a boat under sail.

    (b) He is familiar with a lifeboat and its equipment, and with the starting and running of the engine of a power boat.

    (c) He is familiar with the various methods of launching liferafts, and with precautions to be taken before and during launching, methods of boarding and survival procedure.

Issue of A.B. Certificate

Successful candidates are issued with a Certificate of

Qualification as Efficient Deck Hand. After completing a further two years at sea, in addition to the initial qualifying period for E.D.H., a seaman can apply for the issue of an A.B. Certificate.

Examination During Training Course

The qualifying examination can also be taken by boys who attend a pre-training course at the National Sea Training School at Gravesend. The examination is held before a boy goes to sea, but a qualifying certificate is not issued until the successful candidate has completed the appropriate sea service and obtained the steering certificate as required by all other candidates.

Time, Watches and Bells

Time at sea is based on the four figure notation reckoning from midnight (0000 hours) throughout the twenty-four hours of the day. The day at sea is divided into six watches and bells are struck indicating times at each half hour of each watch (see pages 21 and 22).

Dog Watches

Dog watches are not now a common practice. In fact, on the average ship they are unknown, but in cases where they do operate, then it may be worthwhile to note that dog watches are formed by splitting the evening watch (4 p.m.—8 p.m.) into a first and second dog watch, i.e. 1600—1800 hours and 1800—2000 hours respectively. If the dog watch system is used the bells are struck in the two watches as follows:

Watches	Time	Bells	Watches	Time	Bells
	Midnight	8		1200 hrs.	8
	0030 hrs.	1		1230 ,,	1
	0100 ,,	2		1300 ,,	2
Middle	0130 ,,	3	Afternoon	1330 ,,	3
Watch	0200 ,,	4	Watch	1400 ,,	4
	0230 ,,	5		1430 ,,	5
	0300 ,,	6		1500 ,,	6
	0330 ,,	7		1530 ,,	7
(3.45 a.m.)	0345 ,,	1	(3.45 p.m.)	1545 ,,	1
	0400 hrs.	8		1600 hrs.	8
	0430 ,,	1		1630 ,,	1
	0500 ,,	2		1700 ,,	2
	0530 ,,	3		1730 ,,	3
Morning	0600 ,,	4	Evening	1800 ,,	4
Watch	0630 ,,	5	Watch	1830 ,,	5
	0700 ,,	6		1900 ,,	6
	0730 ,,	7		1930 ,,	7
(7.45 a.m.)	0745 ,,	1	(7.45 p.m.)	1945 ,,	1
	0800 hrs.	8		2000 hrs.	8
	0830 ,,	1		2030 ,,	1
	0900 ,,	2		2100 ,,	2
	0930 ,,	3		2130 ,,	3
Forenoon	1000 ,,	4	First	2200 ,,	4
Watch	1030 ,,	5	Watch	2230 ,,	5
	1100 ,,	6		2300 ,,	6
	1130 ,,	7		2330 ,,	7
(11.45 a.m.)	1145 ,,	1	(11.45 p.m.)	2345 ,,	1

	Time	Bells		Time	Bells
First Dog Watch	1600 hrs.	8	Second Dog Watch	1830 hrs.	1
	1630 „	1		1900 „	2
	1700 „	2		1930 „	3
	1730 „	3		1945 „	1
	1800 „	4		2000 „	8

It will be noted that a quarter of an hour before the end of each watch one bell is struck. This is a general practice at sea to indicate time to the new watch coming on. This does not apply to the dog watch.

Striking Time Bells

The strokes, which should be made away from and back to the body, not from side to side, must be fairly quick double rings. For instance, to 'make' five bells strike twice quickly, pause for a second or so, strike twice quickly again, pause, then strike one. Time bells only are struck in this manner.

Note: Seamen should always use the term to 'make' so many bells. It is incorrect to say 'ring' so many bells.

Men on Watches

Any watchkeeper normally works one watch and is then off duty for the next two watches, i.e. a man on, say, the midnight until 4 a.m. watch will be off duty from 4 a.m. until 12 noon and on again from noon until 1600 hours.

The catering department is the exception to the watch system, its duties commencing daily shortly before breakfast and ceasing after the clearing away of the evening meal.

Watches usually come into force a few hours before a vessel sails and are continued until watches are 'broken' on arrival at the port of destination. Generally speaking, the watch system is disbanded in port so that all the seamen can be employed during daylight hours on jobs of general maintenance. One man, however, from each department is usually placed on permanent nightwatchman duty in port.

Men not on Watch at Sea

Men not appointed to work in watches are known as 'dayworkers' and their general hours of duty are from 7 a.m. until 5 p.m., excluding Saturday afternoons and Sundays. In the deck department these men assist the Boatswain and Carpenter in their jobs of maintaining the ship and her equipment, and in rigging, scaling and painting (Chapter 2).

The Duties of the Deck Watch

In charge of each watch is a Deck Officer and working with him are three seamen (usually two able seamen and one ordinary seaman). During their watch of four hours the officer navigates, plots the position of the ship on the chart and checks the compasses. He is also responsible to the Captain for

(a) seeing that the steering wheel is manned by a good helmsman and a steady course is maintained;

(b) keeping one man on lookout duties;

(c) having one man working within earshot of the bridge so that he may be summoned quickly if needed. This man's duties also include keeping galley fires burning at night and making sure the following watch is called out promptly.

The duties can be summed up thus: wheel, lookout and standby duties.

Let us take three seamen and call them A, B and C. Between them this is how they will split up their duties hourly:

	A	B	C
First Hour	Wheel	Lookout	Standby
Second „	Wheel	Standby	Lookout
Third „	Standby	Wheel	Lookout
Fourth „	Lookout	Wheel	Standby

In this case A's duty is called 'First Wheel', B's duty 'Second Wheel' and C, who has two periods of 'Standby', is called 'Farmer'. (The origin of this nautical slang is not determined.) Every watch A, B and C all move up one; A then takes B's place, B takes C's place and C takes A's place, and so on from watch to watch so that each man in the watch has a fair share of the various duties.

Terms Describing Position and Direction

Generally speaking, any floor upon which one can walk is termed a *Deck,* the walls of any compartment, however large or small, are *Bulkheads* and any ceilings or overheads are known as *Deckheads*.

The right-hand side of a ship is termed the *Starboard* side and the left-hand side the *Port* side.

The starboard side is always associated with the colour green and the port side with the colour red (Chapter 4). The back of a ship is known as the *Stern*, the extreme front end as the *Stem*, and immediately behind the stem is an area called the *Bows*. The central portion of the ship is known as *Amidships*, and that part of the *Main Deck* in front of amidships is called the *Foredeck* and behind it the *Afterdeck*. The external body of the ship below the main deck is referred to as the *Hull* and anything erected above the main deck is termed *Superstructure* (see Fig. 1).

Look at Fig. 1 again and in imagination place

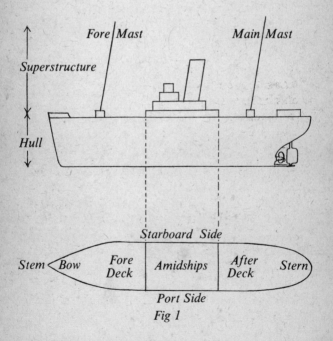

Fig 1

yourself anywhere you choose on the ship, facing the bows. In this position any object in front is said to be *Forward* (pronounced for'ard) of you and any object behind is *Aft* of you. The word *Abaft,* which must not be confused with aft, also means behind, but in a sense generally relative only to objects; for instance, referring to Fig. 1 again, note the funnel is abaft the foremast but forward of the mainmast.

It is essential before proceeding further to thoroughly grasp the meaning of these terms. They are in constant use amongst seamen, and we shall need to make many references to them in the following chapters.

Ships

Types

In the vast number of vessels that compose our mercantile fleet it is true to say that no two ships are identical. Like human beings, they come in all shapes and sizes. These vessels transport our exports to every corner of the globe, returning with food and raw materials. The cargo a ship carries determines her type. There are three main types, the most important of which is the general cargo ship or freighter. This type of ship, which composes the bulk of our fleet, may transport anything of a general nature, including livestock.

Second in importance are ships known as tankers. These ships, which are easily distinguished by the fact that their funnel is fitted astern, are engaged in the carriage of bulk liquid cargoes such as petroleum, oils, etc.

Finally, there are the liners catering almost solely

for passengers, although some of them also carry a certain amount of general cargo and/or mail.

The General Cargo Ship

When building a vessel of this type, a framework is first erected, similar in many ways to the human framework. The backbone of a ship is represented by the keel and the ribs by frames (see Fig. 2b). This framework is then covered by a skin of steel plates, which is referred to generally as the hull. A very important feature of the ship is that the bottom has a double skin and the space in between these two skins forms a series of tanks along the whole length of the ship. These tanks are called Double Bottom Tanks and are used either for carrying oil fuel or water ballast. (Ballast is necessary when a ship is not carrying cargo and needs some weight in her to sink her down far enough for the propeller to 'bite' effectively in the water.) Having a second skin on the bottom of a ship makes her a great deal safer too, as would be obvious in the event of her striking some underwater obstruction.

A glance at Fig. 2a will show you that the bulk of the ship's interior is devoted to cargo space, and that this space is divided up into what are known as Tween Decks and Lower Holds, each one numbered. The bulkheads dividing each of these compartments are rather special in that each one is perfectly water-tight, thus still further increasing the safety factor in the event of stranding or collision, as mentioned in the last paragraph.

Note: The water-tight bulkheads at the extreme ends of the vessel, i.e. the front of No. 1 hold and the back of No. 5 hold, are specially strengthened and

Fig. 2a

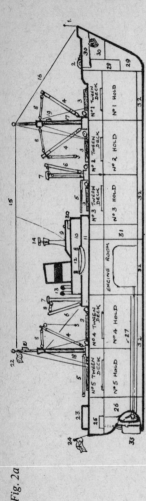

1. Jackstaff
2. Windlass
3. Cargo Hatches
4. Derricks (working position)
5. Derricks (stowed position)
6. Heavy Lift Derricks
7. Sampson Posts
8. Derrick Topping Lifts
9. Navigating Bridge
10. Officers' Accommodation
11. Crew Accommodation
12. Lifeboat
13. Engine Room Ventilators
14. Radar Scanner
15. Main Aerial
16. Fore Stay
17. Foremast
18. Mainmast
19. Fore Steaming Light
20. Starboard Navigation Light
21. Main Steaming Light
22. House Flag
23. Docking Bridge
24. Ensign Staff
25. Steering Engine
26. After Peak Tank
27. Propeller Shaft Tunnel
28. Cable Locker
29. Fore Peak Tank
30. Store Rooms
31. Deep Tank
32. Double Bottom Tanks
33. Rudder

are called the fore and after collision bulkheads respectively.

In the bows and stern of the vessel are compartments for carrying fresh water. These compartments are really large tanks, the one in the bows being known as the Fore Peak Tank and the one in the stern as the After Peak Tank. These tanks are often used—sometimes in conjunction with the double bottom tanks—for 'trimming the ship'. This term means the transferring of water, or sometimes oil fuel in the case of the double bottom tanks, from one compartment to another in order that the ship may be

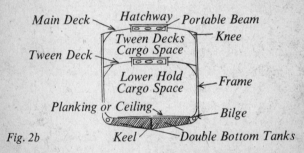

Fig. 2b

kept perfectly upright in the water and not leaning over to one side (listed), or with her bows pressing too far down into the water. It should be mentioned that it is generally desirable for the ship to be 'trimmed a little by the stern', i.e. with the bows a foot or so higher out of the water, and the propeller properly submerged. In the engine room are pumps and valves which allow the transfer of water or oil from one compartment to another.

Running from the bottom of the engine room to the propeller, underneath Nos. 4 and 5 lower holds, is a tunnel formed of steel plates. This tunnel houses the propeller shaft, and there is also room enough for a man to walk along and inspect or oil this shaft.

It will be noticed that between the engine room and No. 4 lower hold is a compartment marked Deep Tank. A deep tank can be filled with water and used as a ballast or trimming tank, but it is often used to carry a small amount of special liquid cargo—linseed oil for instance.

The Tanker

The original design of a ship for transporting crude-oil or petroleum in bulk has altered little over the years, but the modern tanker is a sophisticated unit with complex equipment which, in the future, will undoubtedly include nuclear-power and computerisation.

Until quite recently, tankers were built to a 'three island' design, with a forecastle, an amidships structure and a poop, the three being connected by a fore-and-aft gangway called a 'flying bridge'.

Now they are built to 'all-aft' design – with accommodation, navigation and other spaces being located aft above the ship's engines, machinery and boiler rooms.

Besides being much easier to build, safer and more economical, the construction avoids a long propeller shaft running through the cargo space and trunk which would be difficult to keep oil-tight.

The oil is carried in oil-tight compartments or tanks extending for approximately three-quarters of the length of the ship. The tanks are formed by athwartship and longitudinal bulkheads which, besides adding strength, ensure stability by reducing the free surface of the liquid cargo and also segregating

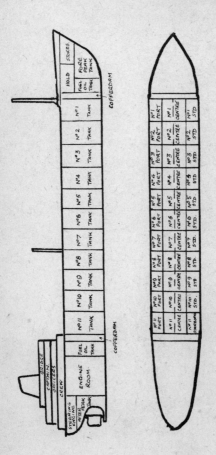

Fig 3a

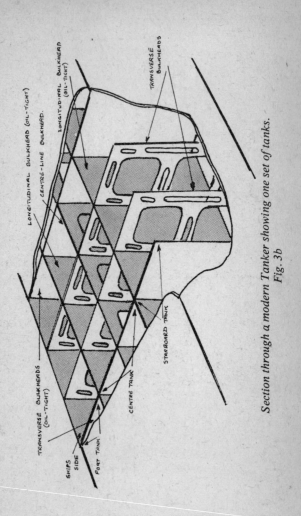

Section through a modern Tanker showing one set of tanks.
Fig. 3b

the different grades of oil. An additional bulkhead at the forward and after ends of the cargo tanks forms cofferdams to isolate the cargo from the ship's own oil fuel tanks and pumping equipment.

The cargo is loaded either by gravity or by shore pumps through large flexible hoses connected to the shore pipe-lines, but discharging is carried out by the ship's own pumps.

Different pipe-line systems are fitted in the tankers depending on the type of cargo carried. Ships carrying various grades of oil have direct pipe-lines from the pump rooms to each set of tanks or a ring-main system for a group of tanks. The flow of oil through the pipes situated at the bottom of the tanks is controlled by sluice valves operated from the main deck levels. The oil is pumped from each tank to the pump room on the suction principle and then by pressure upwards to the deck pipes, manifold to which the flexible shore pipes are connected.

Most modern large crude-oil tankers, which usually carry one grade of oil, operate on a free-flow system; the oil flows through valved openings in the tank bulkheads and, as the oil is pumped from the aftermast tank, it is replaced by the flow of oil from the other tanks. The flow of oil from forward to aft causes the ship to develop a stern trim, and this aids the flow of oil towards the main suction in the after tank.

When the tanker completes the discharge of cargo, selected tanks are used to take on water ballast to keep the ship in a seaworthy condition and manageable on the return trip to the loading port. The remaining tanks are cleaned during the passage in readiness for the next cargo of oil. The discharge of contaminated water used during the cleaning process into the sea may cause pollution of beaches and injury to marine life. This has led several companies to introduce a system which helps to solve the oil pollution problem. Instead of discharging the contaminated water into the sea, the procedure allows all the sludges from the tank washings to be pumped into one slop tank. The next cargo is loaded on top of the washings and discharged at the unloading port to be separated in the refinery.

Bulk Carriers

Other ships which have been built for specialised jobs and have some of the characteristics of the tanker are the bulk carriers. Built mainly to meet the requirement of iron ore by the steel manufacturers, they now operate in other trades as well; sugar, grain, phosphates, etc., are now invariably transported in bulk. Unloading ports have special dockside installations for the rapid discharging of this type of cargo direct from the holds.

Container Ships

In recent years, ships have been designed and purpose built to specialise in the handling and transporting of containers.

Containers are specially made boxes of standard dimensions used by the manufacturer to load his own products at the factory, and then to transport and ship them to the purchaser, who will open and remove the contents. The cargo within the container is not subjected to any individual handling during transportation.

The container ships are fitted with special lifting

appliances for the efficient handling and stowage of the containers. The containers have standard design corner fittings used when lifting and also interlock together when they are loaded into the hold or stowed as deck cargo.

Early methods of handling 'unitised' cargo on a smaller scale compared with containers have now been improved, and ships are being built with side doors through which the cargo is conveyed by fork-lift trucks or roller-conveyors. On a number of cross-Channel ships, loaded trucks are driven aboard through special doors at the bows or stern and drive off at their destination port. Cross-Channel train and car ferries utilise the same method.

The Passenger Liner

No one diagram can do justice to the variety in size and shape of these vessels. Their being called liners implies both their type and purpose. They are generally distinguished from other vessels by having much more superstructure (usually painted white) and very often they have more than one funnel.

CHAPTER 2

ROPE WORK

Although the amount of rope work in a ship has greatly decreased since the days of sail, a seaman still works with rope, and the various methods of handling and using rope have changed little over the years. The techniques used by the seaman in the old 'wooden walls' have survived the test of time and are still used today, be it in the smallest boat or the largest liner.

Only the rope itself has moved along on progressive lines in its type and manufacture, and today rope of all kinds can be classified as belonging to one of three main types:

1. Rope manufactured from vegetable fibre.
2. Rope made of synthetic or man-made fibre.
3. Rope constructed of steel wire.

Vegetable Fibre Rope

The fibre used in the manufacture of a rope depends mainly on the use for which the rope is intended. The main fibres used are as follows:

Manila. Named after the port in the Philippine Islands from where it is exported, this rope is made from the fibre which covers the stalk and leaf of the Abaca plant. It forms a strong, pliable and easy to work rope with a smooth, glossy appearance. It is impervious to salt water and is very suitable for mooring ropes, boat's falls and slings.

Hemp. This rope is made from the fibres of the hemp plant, and is imported from many Eastern and European countries. It manufactures into a soft, strong, flexible rope, but has been superseded by manila in the larger sized ropes and is now used mainly for the smaller lines.

Sisal. Derived from the leaf of a member of the cactus family, this rope is hairy and rough to the hands. It is not as reliable as manila and becomes difficult to handle when wet.

Coir. The fibres forming this rope are obtained from the coconut husk. It is the weakest of all other ropes, but it is very light and springy and floats on water. It is easily recognised by its brown colour and hairy texture.

Cotton. Ropes made of cotton fibres will usually only be found on yachts and similar vessels; their use aboard ship is very limited.

Manufacture of Vegetable Fibre Rope

After cleaning, the fibre threads are first twisted into yarns and the 'spinning' process can be either right- or left-handed. A number of yarns, depending upon the size of rope required, are then twisted together to form strands, the twist usually being in the opposite direction to the twist of the yarns. The rope is then completed by twisting together three or four strands according to the type of rope required. This last twist (known as 'laying') is always in the opposite direction to the twist of the strands. Most ropes have a quantity of lubricant added during the twisting process and are said to be 'oil-spun'. Exceptions to this are referred to as 'dry-spun'.

The 'Lay' of the Rope

The lay of a rope refers to the direction in which the strands of the rope are 'laid-up' or twisted. All ropes in common use are normally three-stranded rope laid up right-handed, i.e. when viewed from above the strands twist in a right-handed spiral. This is the commonest form of lay and is known as *Hawser-laid Rope*.

Four-stranded rope laid up right-handed round a centre heart of the same material is known as *Shroud-laid Rope*.

Three lengths of hawser-laid rope laid up together in the opposite direction to their own lay to form a nine-stranded rope is known as *Cable-laid Rope*.

Rope is said to be *Hard-laid* or *Soft-laid* according to the amount of twist given to the strands during the process of laying.

Rope Measurement and Breaking Strains

All rope is measured for size by its circumference and the breaking strain varies with the size. The manufacturers usually supply a table giving the details of breaking strains for various types and sizes of rope; but a rough method of finding the breaking strain of hemp, sisal or manila is to square its size and divide by 3, the answer being in tons, i.e. for a 2-inch rope:

$$\frac{2 \times 2}{3} = 1\frac{1}{3} \text{ tons.}$$

A safe working load would be to take one-sixth of this value, and this allows for a good margin of safety. The formula applies only to new rope and will decrease as the rope is used.

Miscellaneous Ropes

Square Line. Extensively used as mooring ropes, this type of rope is made up of four pairs of strands plaited in pairs to form a flexible square rope which does not kink. The manufacturers supply special instructions on the splicing of this type of rope.

Log Line. Used exclusively for towed logs, it is made of hemp yarns plaited together, resulting in a flexible, unkinkable and untwistable rope.

Boltrope. This is soft-laid, well stretched rope made of three-stranded hemp. It is soft and pliable, and is used for edging sails and awnings.

Small Stuff. Most cordage under 1 inch in size is referred to as 'small stuff'. This includes spunyarn, marline, houseline, boatlacing and various types of twine and fishing lines.

Man-made Fibre Rope

Synthetic fibres obtained by chemical process have resulted in ropes being made of nylon, terylene and polypropolene, all of which are now widely used in ships. They are superior in strength and flexibility compared with their natural fibre counterparts. Man-made fibre rope will stretch over one-third its own length before breaking and has excellent recovery powers after extension. It is almost non-inflammable and can be stowed away wet without fear of rotting. However, synthetic fibre ropes are affected by acids and alkalines, and can lose strength when exposed to sunlight over long periods. Nylon rope is the most favoured of the synthetic fibres and is used in ships where there is a requirement for heavy duty ropes, such as towing and mooring hawsers.

Steel Wire Rope

Wire rope performs various functions on a modern ship and its manufacture depends largely on the duty for which it is intended to be used. Wire used for standard rigging would be unsuitable as a cargo runner, and it is useful to a seaman to know how this difference comes about. With few exceptions, all wire rope used at sea is made up of six strands; each strand is constructed of a number of small wires running continuously throughout its whole length and twisted left-handed around a wire or jute core. The rope is then formed by laying up the strands right-handed around a jute, hemp or synthetic fibre core. The centre core is usually impregnated with oil during manufacture which lubricates the wires during use. Standing rigging invariably consists of wire rope in which the strands are made up around a wire core and the strands laid up to form the rope around a jute core. Flexibility for running rigging, i.e. cargo runners, boat falls, berthing wires, etc., is obtained by substituting the wire core of the strands for a fibre core and increasing the number of wires in the strands by small gauge wire.

Protection of Special Ropes

Certain ropes on a ship may need to be protected against chafe. This is done in three stages as follows:

1. *Worming*. The lay, in between the strands of the rope, is filled up with small stuff so as to

make the rope's surface smooth and round.

2. *Parcelling*. Strips of canvas or burlap 2-3 inches wide are wrapped around the rope, covering the worming and working in the same direction as the lay.

3. *Serving*. To finish off, the parcelling is then bound tightly with 'spun yarn' working against the lay. (Spun yarn is two, three or four strands twisted together and treated with Stockholm tar for preservation.) The serving or binding can, if necessary, be done by hand, but it is more often done with the aid of a mallet which has a head grooved to fit the rope and is known as a serving mallet (Fig. 4).

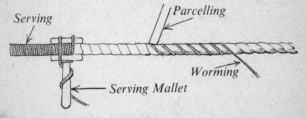

Serving

Parcelling

Worming

Serving Mallet

Fig 4

The rhyme and aid to memory often quoted at sea for the above is:

'Worm and parcel with the lay, turn and serve the other way'.

Preservation of Ropes

The hawsers used for tying a vessel up in port (generally referred to as mooring ropes) are very valuable ropes and great care is taken to ensure their long life. In port they are kept clear of steel decks by wooden gratings, and at sea they are stowed away from the weather, usually in a space reserved for them in the nearest tween deck. Occasionally at sea in sunny weather they are taken out to be aired and dried. No vegetable fibre ropes should be placed away wet as dry rot may set in. Any exposed ropes on the ship which tighten up with wet weather should be temporarily slackened off to prevent strain or breaking.

Knots, Bends and Hitches

The following are the more commonly used knots and their uses which the young seaman is required to know when qualifying for the E.D.H. examination:

Reef Knot: The most common method of joining two ropes of equal size together (Fig. 5).

Sheep Bend: Used to secure a rope's end to a small eye or joining two ropes of unequal size (Fig. 6).

Double Sheep Bend: Used as above when the rope is slippery (Fig. 7).

Clove Hitch: Used to secure a rope's end to a spar or rail where the pull is direct (Fig. 8).

Rolling Hitch: This hitch is used for securing a rope to a spar where the pull is from the side. The two turns are always made on the side which is in the direction of the pull (Fig. 9).

Round Turn and Two Half-hitches: Used to secure a rope to a ring or shackle and also to a heavy spar. It will never jam (Fig. 10).

Bowline: Used for making a temporary eye in the end of a rope (Fig. 11).

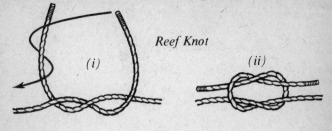

Reef Knot

(i)

(ii)

Fig 5

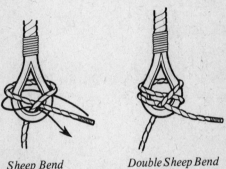

Sheep Bend
Fig 6

Double Sheep Bend
Fig 7

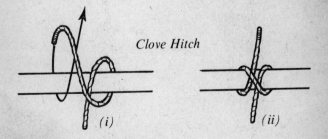

Clove Hitch

(i)

(ii)

Fig 8

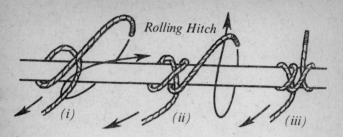

Rolling Hitch

(i)   *(ii)*   *(iii)*

Fig 9

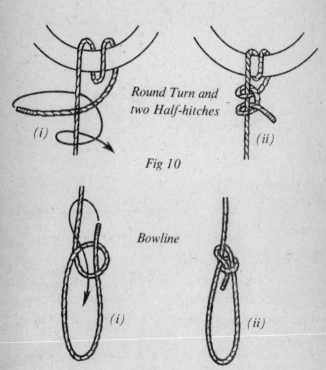

Round Turn and two Half-hitches

(i)   *(ii)*

Fig 10

Bowline

(i)   *(ii)*

Fig 11

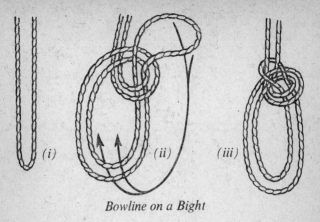

(i)   *(ii)*   *(iii)*

Bowline on a Bight

Fig 12

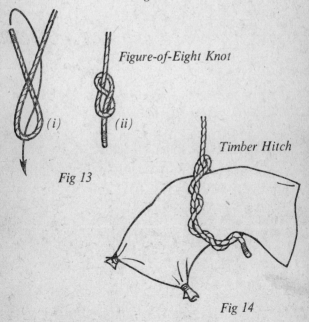

Figure-of-Eight Knot

(i)   *(ii)*

Fig 13

Timber Hitch

Fig 14

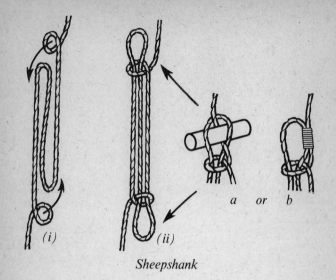

(i) *(ii)* *a* *or* *b*

Sheepshank

Fig 15

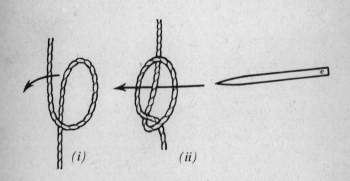

(i) *(ii)*

Marline Spike Hitch

Fig 16

Bowline on the Bight: This is used for lowering a man over the side or from aloft (Fig. 12).

Figure-of-Eight Knot: Made in the end of a rope to prevent it unreeving through a block or eye (Fig. 13).

Timber Hitch: Used when hoisting filled sacks or large spars (Fig. 14).

Sheepshank: Used for temporarily shortening a length of rope (Fig. 15).

Whippings

To stop the end of a rope from fraying, the ends are whipped, i.e. bound tightly together with twine. There are three methods of whipping as follows:

1. *Common Whipping* (Fig. 17)
This method is fast and easy, and results in a strong, neat whipping. It is the most frequently used of the three. To make a common whipping proceed as follows:

Form a loop with an end of twine and place this on the rope to be whipped. Then, taking the long end of the twine, bind it tightly around both rope and loop working away from the end. When about half an inch of binding has been put on, place the long end through the loop. To finish off, pull the short end of twine so that the loop comes about midway underneath the whipping and cut off the ends. Another method of common whipping is to bind the twine around the rope for about a quarter of an inch before forming a loop and finish off as described above.

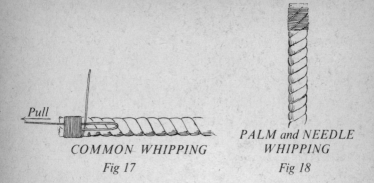

COMMON WHIPPING
Fig 17

PALM and NEEDLE
WHIPPING
Fig 18

2. *Palm and Needle Whipping* (Fig. 18)

Rather slower than a common whipping, but just as simple and the strongest and best of the whippings. The name given to this whipping is derived from the fact that sailmaker's tools are needed.

To make a palm and needle whipping proceed as follows:

Using single thread place the needle under one strand and pull through almost the whole length of twine. Bind the twine tightly around the rope for about half an inch working away from the end. Then place the needle under one strand again and pull tight. Come back over the top of the binding, carefully following round the twist of the strands (the lay), and tuck the needle under another strand. Treat each strand of the rope in a similar manner and cut the twine off short, finishing as in Fig. 18.

On large ropes both palm and needle are used to make a palm and needle whipping, but on smaller ropes the palm is often dispensed with.

3. *West Country Whipping*

This whipping is seldom used at sea nowadays. It is rather awkward to make and the finished appearance is generally far from neat. To form a West Country whipping middle the twine and place the rope to be whipped through the loop so formed. Proceed by twisting or half knotting the twine at every half turn, thus forming a row of half knots on opposite sides of the rope. Finish off with a reef knot.

The Sailmaker's Palm

This is simply a strong leather band which is made to run across the palm and around the back of the hand and is looped around the thumb. At the base of the thumb is an indented metal plate which enables the operator to push a needle with considerable force through rope or canvas.

The Sailmaker's Needle

These needles, which are the ones used in rope and canvas work at sea, are different from ordinary needles in that the eyes are larger and the shaft of the needle is always three cornered. There are eleven different sizes numbered from 6 to 16, the largest being a No. 6.

Seizings

When it is necessary to secure two ropes to each other, side by side, then a type of whipping is placed on which seamen term a seizing. There are three types of seizings, as follows:

1. *Round Seizing*

This is used when the stress on both of the ropes which are to be secured side by side is equal.

Commence by splicing an eye in one end of the seizing. Pass the seizing around the two ropes, bring the unspliced end through the eye and heave tight. Now wind the seizing around the two ropes for about six complete turns, pulling tight at each turn. Pass the end back underneath these turns in the space left by the rounds of the rope and bring it out through the eye of the seizing. The binding process is now repeated on top of the original turns, being careful to see that each turn rests in the hollow formed by the two parts of seizing below it. Pass the seizing back underneath the turns as before, bring it out between the two ropes and form a clove hitch (see **Knots**) across the top of the seizing.

2. *Flat Seizing*

The round seizing described above is used when great strength is required, whereas the flat seizing is a much lighter means of securing two ropes.

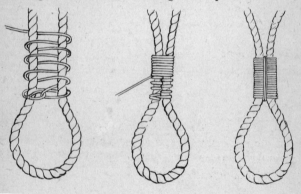

Racking Seizing

Fig 19

To form a flat seizing proceed as for the round seizing, and finish up with a clove hitch after the first set of turns have been completed and the end tucked back through the eye.

3. *Racking Seizing*
This is used when the stress on the ropes which are to be secured is unequal.

Commence by splicing an eye in one end of the seizing, passing the seizing around the two ropes, and bringing the unspliced end back through the eye and heaving tight as in the round or flat seizing. Then, instead of simply winding the seizing around the two ropes as before, dip the seizing back between the two ropes at each half turn, going over and under in figure-of-eight style (see Fig. 19) for about a dozen turns. Pull tight at each turn and when these dozen or so 'racking turns' are completed, go back over them with ordinary turns and finish off in the same manner as a round seizing.

Splicing

If you have given just a little time and thought to your knots, whippings and seizings, you should be agreeably surprised at their simplicity. Splicing a rope is regarded by some as an intricate process performed only by the more experienced seamen. Such is not the case; a good neat splice can be made by anyone after just a few minutes of concentrated application. We shall now deal with three different splices, using three-stranded rope in each case. The more difficult Long Splice can only be taught adequately by practical demonstration—and this also applies to splicing with wire rope.

1. *The Short Splice*

The purpose of this splice is to join two ropes together.

Proceed by taking the two ends to be joined and unlaying the strands in each about three full turns. Now marry the ropes together so that the strands of one lie alternately between the strands of the other. Be careful before proceeding further that you do not have two strands lying together. Have a good look at Fig. 20. The beginner would now be well advised to temporarily seize the strands from (a) rope to (b)

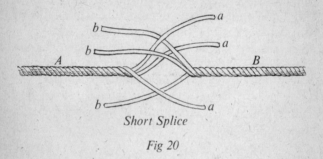

Short Splice

Fig 20

rope. Now, taking any one of (b) strands and working against the lay of the rope, go over one strand and tuck under the next in (a) rope. Now take the next strand to the left of the one just tucked and treat in a similar manner, i.e. over one, under one. Treat the third strand likewise. This completes what is called the first tuck (although actually, of course, we have tucked three separate strands). On the completion of a tuck, each strand of (b) rope should be protruding separately between each strand of (a) rope. If two strands protrude through at one point then the splice is wrong. To finish, give the same three strands

another one or two complete tucks as already
described, then cut the temporary whipping and
splice (a) strands into (b) rope in a similar manner.

2. *Back Splice*

The purpose of the back splice is permanently to
prevent the end of a rope from fraying. Whereas
whippings may have to be replaced occasionally, a
back splice will finish off the rope's end neater and
will last the life of the rope.

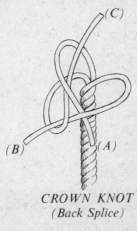

CROWN KNOT
(Back Splice)

Fig 21

Study Fig. 21 closely. The knot that has been
formed loosely by the three strands (A), (B) and (C) is
known as a crown knot. To form a crown knot
proceed as follows:

Unlay the strands about three full turns, then,
holding the rope in front of you with the unlayed
strands uppermost, select the middle strand and call it

(A). Pull (A) down towards you and let your thumb
hold it against the lower part of the rope, leaving a
small loop at the top. Now take the strand furthest to
the right of you and call this (B). Place this one
across and in front of (A) strand so that it projects
out to the left and at right angles to the rope. The
remaining strand ((C) in the diagram) is also pulled
towards you but underneath and around (B) strand
and back through the loop formed by (A).

Tighten this knot by gently pulling on each strand
in turn until it settles tightly on top of the rope. Now
take any strand and, again working against the lay of
the rope (see paragraph on 'The Lay of the Rope'),
place it over the next immediate strand and tuck
under the following one. Keeping the crown knot to
the left, turn the whole rope slightly towards you, and
this will present the next strand to be tucked. This is
treated in a similar manner to the last strand, i.e. over
one, under one. The remaining strand is dealt with in
exactly the same fashion and this completes the first
tuck (as in the short splice). Generally three complete
tucks are quite sufficient for a back splice.

Note: Although it will be understood that each
strand has to be separately tucked, the word 'tuck'
implies that each of the strands (A), (B) and (C) have
been tucked once in order.

3. *The Eye Splice*
If you refer back to your knots for a moment, you
will find that a loop can be made in the end of a rope
by forming a bowline. This loop would only be a
temporary one, and when a more permanent loop or
'eye' is required then the eye splice is employed. A
ship's mooring ropes (see paragraph on 'Preservation

of Ropes') have an eye spliced in each end of them so that they can easily be slipped over the bollards or posts on the quayside when a ship is tying up.

To make an eye splice unlay the end of the rope about three full turns and bend the rope round so as to form a loop of the required size. Select the middle strand ((A) in Fig. 22) and tuck this one against the

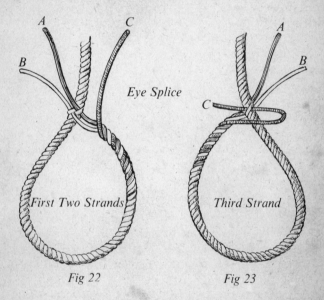

Eye Splice

First Two Strands   *Third Strand*

Fig 22   Fig 23

lay of the rope. Now take the left-hand strand (B) and tuck it against the lay of the rope, making sure that it lies below (A) in the figure. Finally, turn the rope over to the back and tuck (C) strand, from right to left, against the lay of the rope as in Fig. 23. Each of the strands (A), (B) and (C) should now come out separately between each strand of the rope, and completing the splice is now simply a matter of going over one, under one, as in the final stages of both the short and back splice. Three complete tucks are usual with an eye splice.

Sailmaker's Eye Splice

In this splice the strands are tucked with, instead of against, the lay of the rope. It forms a somewhat neater eye, but it should not be used where any strain is likely to bear on the rope or else the splice will 'draw', i.e. come apart.

Hints on Splicing

After tucking a strand, twist it so that the yarns in the strand tighten up and at the same time pull the strand back in the direction where your splice began. If you do this with each strand in turn as you go, the completed splice will be tight and neat. A loose splice should be avoided as it will 'draw' when any weight or strain is applied.

Before splicing rope which exceeds about 3 inches in circumference, it will be found necessary to whip the end of each strand to prevent it from fraying out in the process of splicing. Also with larger ropes it will be found that either a 'marline spike' or a 'fid' is needed to open up each strand in the rope for tucking. A marline spike is simply a hardened piece of steel about 9 inches long and about 1 inch in diameter at one end, tapered down to a point at the other. A fid is a larger edition of a marline spike, but is made of hardwood and is generally used when splicing mooring ropes. A large fid may be 30 inches long and as much as 4 or 5 inches in diameter.

The appearance of any splice can be greatly improved by tapering it. This is done by halving the yarns in each strand after the first tuck, and halving and tucking them again after the second tuck.

Blocks and Tackles

This title may sound slightly reminiscent of sailing ship days, but a glance at a modern ship discharging her cargo would dispel any doubts about it being old fashioned. At least three blocks and tackles are used with every cargo derrick, and a ship may easily have twenty derricks or more.

Blocks

Every block has a shell or outer case which houses the sheave or roller over which the rope travels, and this sheave is kept in place and allowed freedom to revolve by a pin which passes through its centre and is secured to the shell. Wooden blocks are often made stronger by having a heavy iron band fitted around the outside of the block with a metal eye welded to it for attaching to hooks, etc. This is known as an External Bound Block. More common nowadays perhaps is a block known as an Internal Bound Block, and in this case the iron band is partly concealed inside the wooden case of the block. Steel blocks also come in various shapes and sizes, but the best known and the most used in shipboard work are those used for loading or discharging cargo. These blocks, when attached to a cargo derrick, are known as Gins. They have self-lubricating sheaves and are fitted to the derrick by means of a swivel eye. Blocks are measured by the size of the diameter of their sheave.

A block known as a Snatch Block is often met

with too. This is simply a small iron block which has a hinged side. This enables a rope to be placed over the sheave without reeving the end through the block.

Tackles and Purchases

A tackle (pronounced taykel) is simply the use of two blocks and a rope to gain power, i.e. in this case to enable one to move a weight more easily.

Example: Imagine that an engine room ventilator weighing, say, 15 cwt has to be lifted vertically upwards from the deck to be placed in position. One block will have to be secured high above the ventilator and this is known as the Standing Block. The other block will be attached to the ventilator and will be known as the Moving Block. We will select as our tackle a Handy Billy (see Fig. 26). A glance at this will show that there are three parts of rope at the moving block. The number of parts of rope at the moving block in any tackle determines the power it gains, so in this case the power gained is three times, or in other words a weight of 5 cwt (a pull equal to five hundredweight) should theoretically raise our 15 cwt ventilator. The fact that it would not in practice is because we have not made any allowance for frictional resistance. To allow for this count the number of sheaves (in this case three) and add one-tenth for each sheave to the total weight of the ventilator:

i.e. $\frac{1}{10}$ of 15 cwt is 1.5 cwt. Therefore $\frac{3}{10}$ of 15 cwt is 4.5 cwt. 4.5 cwts added to 15 cwt is 19.5 cwts, which equals the total load on the purchase.

We mentioned that the power gained by this purchase was three times; therefore it follows that one-third of the total weight of 19.5 cwt, i.e. 6.5 cwt, is the weight or power which has to be applied to the hauling part of the purchase to raise the 15 cwt ventilator.

This little practical problem can be applied to any weight which has to be lifted with the use of any purchase, as long as the above simple rules are adopted.

Types of Tackles and Purchases

Figs. 24–28 show various types of tackles and purchases in common use aboard the modern ship.

Gun Tackle. Two single hook blocks. The power gained is two or three times, depending upon which is the moving block. If the upper block in the figure is

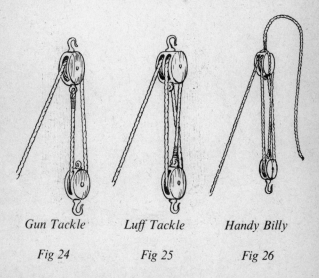

Gun Tackle	Luff Tackle	Handy Billy
Fig 24	Fig 25	Fig 26

the moving block, then the tackle is said to be rove to advantage and the power gained is three times; but if the lower block is the moving block, then the tackle is rove to disadvantage and the power gained is only twice.

Luff Tackle. A double and a single hook block. Rove to advantage the power gained is 4, and rove to disadvantage, 3.

Handy Billy. A double block with a rope tail and a single block with a hook. Rove to advantage the power gained is 4, and rove to disadvantage, 3.

Double Luff. Two double hook blocks. Rove to advantage the power gained is 5, and to disadvantage, 4.

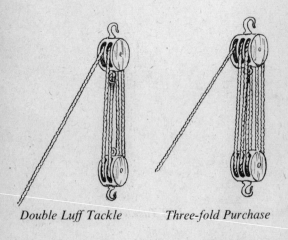

Double Luff Tackle   *Three-fold Purchase*

Fig 27   *Fig 28*

Three-fold Purchase. Two three-fold blocks. Rove to advantage the power gained is 7, and to disadvantage, 6.

Note: There are also four-, six- and eight-fold purchases for heavier work.

CHAPTER 3

COMPASS AND STEERING

General

Imagine for a moment that this country is suddenly plunged into total darkness, that you are placed in some new and completely strange locality, and from there you have to find your way home. You would be lost in the true sense of the word, with no sense of direction. A ship at sea never loses her sense of direction, although out of sight of land and with perhaps sun, moon and stars completely obscured. Night and day she plods steadily onwards towards her destination. That destination may be hundreds or perhaps thousands of miles away, but it is reached with almost uncanny accuracy. The ship's sense of direction is her compass, and a seaman's faith in this instrument must be complete and founded on a sound knowledge of its construction, function and peculiarities, and limitations.

Types of Compasses

There are two types of compasses in use at sea with slight variations of each. They are the Magnetic or Mariner's Compass and the Gyro Compass.

The Magnetic or Mariner's Compass

This type of compass, as the name implies, depends upon the magnetism of the Earth itself for its direction-finding properties. Let us think of the world for a moment before going on. We know that it is nearly a sphere and that it revolves about an imaginary axis which terminates in two points, one being called the North Pole and the other the South Pole. These points are called the True North Pole or the True South Pole of the Earth. A mariner's compass does not point to the true north or south and we shall now discover why.

The Earth as a Magnet. A magnet is weakest in the middle and strongest at the ends or poles, and if an ordinary bar magnet or a compass needle is balanced on a pivot, the end of the bar or needle which points northwards is termed the 'North Seeking End' and the other the 'South Seeking End'. With two magnets it will be found that, if the two 'North Seeking Ends' or the two 'South Seeking Ends' are brought close together, they will repel each other, whereas the ends of opposite names will be strongly attracted.

The Earth itself possesses magnetic qualities and it can be imagined that a huge bar magnet runs through it, with the ends terminating in two points—one being called the Magnetic North Pole and the other the Magnetic South Pole. Unfortunately, this imaginary bar magnet does not coincide with the Earth's axis, and its ends, or poles, terminate more than a thousand miles from the true North and South Poles. Thus it is to a position in the extreme north of Canada that the North Seeking End of a compass needle is attracted, while the South Seeking End points to a spot on the edge of the Antarctic Continent due south of Tasmania.

Note: It states in the first paragraph that the like ends of two magnets repel each other and this appears to be contradicted by the second paragraph which mentions that the *North* Seeking End of a compass needle is attracted to the Magnetic *North* Pole. The explanation of this is that, if the Earth be considered as a magnet, the South Seeking End is that which is termed the Magnetic North Pole.

We have established then that there are two North Poles to the Earth, the True North Pole and the other to which the compass needle of a magnetic or mariner's compass points, namely the Magnetic North Pole. We shall refer to these poles again shortly.

Construction. The compass card itself is circular in shape, about 8 in in diameter, and is marked off around the edge in degrees and points of the compass. Two or more magnetised needles are attached to its underside, and the whole card is balanced on a pivot and supported in a compass bowl. The bowl is filled with a mixture of alcohol and water, which helps to keep the card steady when the ship is rolling. (The alcohol is used to prevent the water from freezing.)

This compass bowl is supported in a wooden stand called a *Binnacle* by means of a ring which is free to move about a horizontal axis and is attached to both the binnacle and the compass bowl. This system of suspension is known as a *Gimbal Ring,* and it allows the compass bowl to remain level and reasonably steady, however unsteady the ship and binnacle may be. The binnacle is usually provided with a brass dome-shaped cover.

On each side of the binnacle (see Fig. 29) is a large soft iron *Sphere* and in front is a brass encased cylindrical-shaped iron bar known as the *Flinders Bar*. It is sufficient to say that these components, in conjunction with certain magnets which will be found low in the binnacle case, are used in counteracting

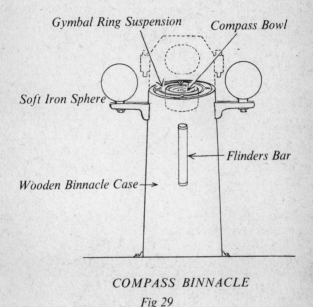

Gymbal Ring Suspension   *Compass Bowl*

Soft Iron Sphere

Flinders Bar

Wooden Binnacle Case →

COMPASS BINNACLE

Fig 29

the effect of the steel in the ship on the compass. They should never be touched by anyone except a certified compass adjuster, or a ship's officer who has his Captain's permission. Here may be a good place to add that a helmsman, before taking over the wheel, should make sure that he has no iron or steel on his person in the way of knives, watches, etc., as this can, in some cases, seriously deflect the compass needle away from Magnetic North.

Errors. There are very few instruments made without an error of some kind and the mariner's compass is no exception. However, being aware of the error we can often do something about correcting it, and if it is a permanent error we can allow for it in our calculations. There are two errors in the compass which affect the seaman; one is a permanent error, and the other temporary and dependent upon circumstances.

Variation. The permanent error in all magnetic compasses is that, instead of pointing to the True Pole of the Earth, they point to the Magnetic Pole. This error we call *Variation,* and if you think about it a little you will realise that the angle of variation itself depends upon your position on the Earth and the angle you subtend to the two poles. Your variation at any spot on the Earth can be read at a glance from any good chart.

Deviation. The temporary error that affects all magnetic compasses is known as *Deviation*. Deviation is a very elusive amount, so much so that on the seagoing ship the officer of the watch has to calculate and perhaps allow for it from hour to hour. This error arises from the effect of steel in the ship, and the nature of her cargo and how it is distributed, and can also be seriously affected by, say, a change in position of the ship's cranes or derricks.

A combination of variation and deviation gives us what is known as the *Compass Error,* and this must be allowed for when setting a course.

The Gyro Compass

This is an ingenious precision instrument which is entirely independent of the Earth's magnetism. It is electrically operated and points to the True North Pole.

The principle of this instrument is the Gyroscope. A gyroscope is simply a flywheel mounted on a spindle, which is free not only to rotate but to move about both the horizontal and the vertical axes. Newton's first law of motion states that **every body continues in its state of rest or of uniform motion in a straight line, unless it is compelled by forces to change that state.** If we apply that law to a gyroscope, i.e. a freely spinning wheel, it may be expressed by stating that a freely spinning wheel tends to maintain the direction of its plane of rotation in space and, of course, the direction of its axis in space. What we do, in fact, is to bring the axis of our gyro compass parallel to the Earth's axis. Once this is achieved, the above law will apply and our gyroscope, which has now become our gyro compass, will point constantly in this direction, and give us True North and South. It should be stated that the rather broad principle described above is combined with two constant, natural phenomena: that of the Earth's rotation and the force of gravity.

The high speed flywheel and its numerous component parts are mounted in a case, the whole being known as the Master Compass. From the master compass to various parts of the ship radiate electrically operated gyro compass repeaters.

Positions of Compasses in the Ship

According to the position of a compass in the ship,

so it is named. The most important compass is one known as the *Standard Compass* and this is usually situated in the highest part of the ship amidships. It is important that there should be an unrestricted all-round view of the horizon from this compass as it is used for taking bearings of shore objects and other ships, and observations of heavenly bodies for the purpose of calculating the compass error. Beneath this compass, in an enclosed compartment known as the wheel house, is another compass which the helmsman uses to steer by. This is known simply as the *Steering Compass*. In the stern of the ship is another compass similar to the two previously mentioned which is only brought into use in the event of emergency. This is known as the *Emergency Steering Compass*. A miniature compass is carried in each of a ship's lifeboats.

All the above compasses are the magnetic type.

A gyro compass when carried operates best when it can be placed fairly low in the vessel amidships. Here it is least affected by the rolling, pitching and vibration of the ship.

Boxing the Compass

The compass card is divided into the 360 degrees of a circle, and nowadays the order to the helmsman to steer a certain course is usually given in degrees. In other words, a course is simply given to him verbally as a number. This is known as the three figure notation of steering, north being either 0 or 360 degrees, east 90 degrees, south 180 degrees, west 270 degrees and so on back to north.

In addition to being divided into degrees, the

compass card is also marked around the edge at $11\frac{1}{4}$ degree intervals by points. This gives us a total of 32 points to the compass, and the term 'boxing the compass' means the ability to recognise immediately the position on the compass card of any given point. To be able to do this it is necessary to memorise thoroughly all the 32 points. Four points of the compass which are recognised by all are, of course, north, south, east and west. These are the most important points and are known as the *Cardinal Points*. Half way between each of these points are the secondary points, north-east, north-west, south-east and south-west. These are the *Half-cardinal Points*. Midway between each cardinal and half-cardinal are points known as *Three-letter Points*. These are named after the cardinal and half-cardinal, which they lie between; the cardinal, being most important, is always named first. Therefore, working clockwise from north, these form the points: NNE, ENE, ESE, SSE, SSW, WSW, WNW, NNW. This gives us a total so far of 16 points, and the 16 remaining points lie midway between each of the points already mentioned and are called *By Points*.

In Fig. 30 it will be observed that all by points lie midway between either a cardinal or half-cardinal and a three-letter point; notice also that every by point is named after the cardinal or half-cardinal next to it. After the naming of the cardinal or half-cardinal then comes the word 'by', and this is always followed by the naming of the nearest cardinal point to which the by point is inclined.

For example, take the half-cardinal north-east in Fig. 30 and it will be noticed there is a by point on each side of it. In each case the by point is called

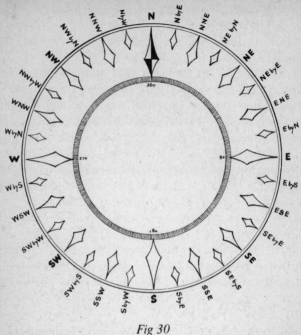

Fig 30

north-east, but the one lying to the north of north-east is termed 'North-east by North' and the one to the east is termed 'North-east by East'. This simple rule applies to all the by points.

Steering Gears

Generally speaking, all vessels are steered by means of a rudder at the stern. The means by which the rudder is controlled depends mostly upon the size and age of the vessel. Roughly they can be divided into three sections:

1. Small craft, i.e. rowing boats, small motor
    boats and sailing craft.
2. Mechanically propelled barges, river craft, etc.
3. Larger coastal and deep sea vessels.

1. *Steering for Small Craft*

Most small craft are steered by means of either a tiller
or a yoke and lines. (A very small boat can also be
steered by an oar placed out over the stern, and in
fact a boat of this type can be both propelled and
steered by a single oar. This is known as sculling a
boat. Sculling is an art which can only be acquired by
actual practice in small boats (Chapter 11).)

2. *Steering for River Craft, etc.*

The methods of steering on these types of craft vary
considerably, but two of the most common are (a) the
direct gearing method and (b) rod and chain steering.

Direct Gearing. In this method the steering wheel is
geared direct to the rudder. The disadvantages of this
method are that the steering wheel has, of course, to
be mounted almost directly above the rudder head
and that the steering wheel itself has to be larger than
is usual to enable a man to get sufficient leverage to
turn it. This type of steering is, however, found on
many inland river craft and especially on vessels
which have no steam or motor power.

Rod and Chain Steering. Not very many years ago,
practically all steam vessels were steered by this
method, and even today there are a number of deep
sea ships and a host of coastal craft which rely on rod
and chain steering. Essentially, the ship must have
steam power because with this method the rudder is

actually turned with a small steam engine. This engine (called the steering engine) is usually situated in a sheltered place in the stern of the ship, and by gearing it is connected to a steel post which runs up through the rudder. To the head of this post, termed the 'Rudder Post', is firmly connected a steel quadrant, the rounded edge of which has teeth gearing that connect with a small cog wheel operated by the engine.

The steering wheel in this case is usually situated amidships, and connection between it and the steering engine is maintained by lengths of steel rod and chain which are bolted together. A valve on the engine is opened or closed according to which way the wheel is turned, the opening of this valve, of course, admitting steam to the engine, which turns the quadrant and rudder. The disadvantages of rod and chain steering are, in the main, the necessary exposure to corrosion and damage of the rods and chains, the noise created when rods or chains pass through living quarters, and the large amount of power wasted in overcoming frictional resistance.

3. *Steering for Larger Vessels*

Most modern ships and almost all deep sea ships are steered by means of hydraulic pressure. In principle, this method is very similar to the rod and chain steering, the main difference being that the steering engine is controlled in this case by liquid which is forced from the steering wheel to the steering engine through two small-diameter copper pipes. On the bridge of the ship the steering wheel is connected to a device known as a steering telemotor. This device is simply two pistons which operate in two liquid-filled cylinders; the base of each cylinder is connected to the two copper pipes previously mentioned. Fitted to the steering engine are two similar pistons and cylinders. When the wheel is turned to starboard, the starboard piston forces liquid along the starboard pipe and operates the piston on the steering engine, which admits steam to the engine and turns the rudder to starboard. The liquid used in this system is either a very light oil or glycerine and water, which in each case is practically non-freezing. The advantages of this method of steering are obvious. The small copper pipes can be led easily and directly to the steering engine, there is less risk of breakdowns or damage, the action of the steering wheel and of the whole system is much smoother, and also, except for the movement of the steering engine, it is quite noiseless.

Emergency Steering. All vessels have to have some alternative method of steering in the event of a breakdown. This varies from ship to ship and is something any intelligent seaman should acquaint himself with on joining a new ship. Generally, it consists of wire ropes and tackles leading from each side of the quadrant in the most convenient way to a winch or windlass.

Steering

The art of steering a ship cannot be learned from a book, and one can only become proficient after considerable practice. There are a few hints, though, which may prevent a beginner from making obvious mistakes. The first and most important thing is to understand the three-figure method of notation and be able to box the compass. The next thing is to have a knowledge of all the helm orders which are likely to be given by the Captain or officer of the watch.

When steering, remember that the ship's head will always turn in the direction in which the wheel is turned, and that when a vessel falls off her course the wheel must be turned in the opposite direction to bring her back again. A person learning to steer often tends to forget that, whereas the ship may be moving a little from side to side, the compass card itself always remains steady. You will be assisted in remembering this by a line, known as the *Lubber Line,* which faces you on the inside of the compass bowl; this line travels around the card when the ship is altering course and represents the true fore and aft line of the ship.

When a ship starts to fall off her course, say to port, the helmsman counteracts this by turning the wheel to starboard sufficient to bring her back on her course again. Often, though, he finds that he has applied a little more wheel than was necessary, and in this case the ship's head will fall off to starboard; this in turn will be corrected by turning the wheel a little to port. When he manages to settle the ship steadily on her course, he places the wheel in the position known as midships, i.e. so that the rudder is in line with the keel. When the vessel falls off again, as she will do according to the state of the sea or wind, the whole process is repeated. The art of a good helmsman is to do this with as little movement of the wheel as possible, the actual amount the wheel is moved depending, of course, upon prevailing weather conditions.

Helm Orders

The steering orders given by the Captain or officer of the watch must be repeated by the helmsman and immediately carried into operation. The following are the orders commonly used at sea:

'Midships'

This order means that the rudder must be placed straight in line with the keel. With telemotor steering this can be done by simply taking your hands off the wheel, and a spring arrangement in the telemotor will automatically level off the liquid in the two pipes, thus bringing the rudder midships. Also, most ships are fitted with a rudder angle indicator which will show you the position of the rudder at any instant.

'Port/Starboard a Bit'

This simply means that you turn the wheel to port or starboard about a half a turn.

'Port/Starboard More'

Very often, after the order 'port' or 'starboard a bit', it may be found that the ship is not swinging fast enough. In this case the order is given to 'port' or 'starboard more'.

'Hard a Port/Starboard'

The order 'hard a port' or 'hard a starboard' means that the wheel is to be put over as far as it will go either to port or starboard.

'Steady as She Goes' or 'Steady'

This order means that the helmsman should look at his compass, and then check the ship from swinging and steady her on the course she was steering when the order was given. After repeating the order 'steady' or 'steady as she goes', it is usual for the helmsman to mention also the course the ship is steering in degrees.

'Ease the Wheel'

Sometimes when the ship is perhaps swinging a little too fast on an alteration of course, the order is given to 'ease the wheel'. This simply means easing the wheel back towards the position of midships, thus stopping the vessel from swinging too quickly.

'How is Her Head'

To this question the helmsman should glance at his compass and if the vessel is on her course reply 'right on, sir', but if she is not on course he should reply by giving the course in degrees the vessel is steering.

A Few Hints on Steering

It will be found that the steering wheel has eight spokes and that one of these has either a brass dome fitted over the top or else three notches cut into the spoke itself. This is known as the midship spoke and it is marked in this way so that the helmsman can make doubly sure his wheel is midships when ordered to do so. It is of considerable value to him at night because he can then steer by feeling the position of the midship spoke. Sometimes the spoke opposite to the midship spoke is also marked to enable the helmsman to know when he has half a turn of wheel on.

A duty at the wheel normally lasts two hours and is known as a 'Trick'. When a man is relieved after a trick at the wheel, he should make quite sure the vessel is steady on her course and if his wheel is midships he should make sure his relief knows this. He should also satisfy himself that the relief knows the course he is to steer, and that he is aware of any peculiarities of wind or weather which may affect the steering of the ship. Before finally leaving the wheelhouse and bridge, the helmsman should report to the officer of the watch the course the ship was steering when he was relieved. For the two hours a man is at the wheel, concentration is imperative; mind wandering can seriously affect a ship's progress, especially in rough weather. Also, a good helmsman should refuse to let distractions, such as another vessel passing or the first sight of land, have any effect on his steering. Talking, of course, is strictly forbidden.

At night, do not have the compass card too brightly illuminated as this will tend to strain the eyes and the steady concentration required may be lost.

CHAPTER 4

THE RULE OF THE ROAD AT SEA

In practically every country in the world there is some system of traffic control. In this country we are all familiar with policemen on point duty, traffic lights, road signs and zebra crossings, etc. All motorists before they are allowed to take a car on the road are required to have passed a driving test, and to do this, in addition to driving, they must have a good knowledge of the contents of a small booklet called the 'Highway Code'.

When a vessel is out of sight of land there are no beacons or lights to aid her, but there is, so to speak, a Highway Code. This code has been adopted by all nations who use the high seas, and it should be carefully read and understood by all aspiring seamen. The code, which relates to the lights carried by and the behaviour of ships at sea, is contained in 31 Rules of International Regulations for the Prevention of Collisions at Sea. These Regulations are printed in full at the end of this book, but before proceeding let us summarise and word them in simple language.

Notice first that the Regulations are divided into two definite sections, Rules 1-16 dealing with lights and fog signals, and Rules 17-31 telling us what action to take under certain circumstances. Notice also that Parts A, C and D are headed by a 'Preliminary', and that an annexe to the Rules is included at the end. Do not skip through these because they are as important as the Regulations.

Part A—Preliminary and Definitions

Rule 1

The rules that follow shall be observed by ships of all nations when they are at sea, or in any channel, river, canal or inland waterway. An exception to this can be made by a local authority when a vessel is being navigated in restricted waters (Rule 30).

Any ship which is mechanically propelled is called a power-driven vessel in these Rules.

Any power-driven vessel which has a sail up (some trawlers for instance) and is not using her engines is classed as a sailing vessel, and any sailing vessel which is using mechanical power is classed as a power-driven vessel.

The term 'under way' means the ship is afloat with no connections of any kind to the shore or the sea bed, e.g. an anchor. Do not confuse the words 'under way' with the term 'making way'. Making way means that the ship is under way and moving through the water.

Part B—Lights Carried by Ships at Sea

Navigation lights shall be shown by ships in all weathers from sunset to sunrise.

Rule 2—A Power-driven Vessel Under Way

Ships of under 150 feet in length carry one and ships over 150 feet two white masthead lights. All power-driven vessels carry a green light on the starboard side, a red light on the port side and a fixed white stern light.

Ships of over 150 feet in length carry the two masthead lights on separate masts, the light on the foremast always being lower than the one on the mainmast. This enables approaching vessels to estimate roughly each other's course.

Rule 3—Vessels Towing

This Rule mainly refers to tugs, but also includes the case of one ship towing another. This type of ship shows two or three white lights according to the length of the tow and the number of ships she is towing. These lights are carried on the same mast, one above the other. She also shows port and starboard lights the same as a power-driven vessel and a small white stern light. By day, if the length of tow exceeds 600 ft, the towing vessel displays a black diamond shape where it can best be seen.

Rule 4(a)—A Vessel 'Not Under Command'

The term 'not under command' means that a ship is unable to manoeuvre in the normal manner. She is hampered perhaps by some breakdown in engines or steering, and all other vessels in the vicinity must give her a wide berth. Being 'not under command' does not mean that a vessel is in distress or that she requires assistance. By day she will show two black balls in a vertical line one over the other and at night she replaces the black balls with red lights. If she is moving through the water, she also shows her red and green sidelights and a stern light.

Rule 4(c)—Cable Layers

A vessel of this type when laying cable in the daytime shows three shapes high up in the ship one over the other. The highest and lowest of these is round in shape and red in colour, and the middle one is diamond shaped and white. At night these shapes are replaced by lights of the same colour as the shapes, and if she is moving through the water she also shows her red and green sidelights and a stern light.

Rule 4(d)—Minesweepers

A vessel engaged in minesweeping operations by day displays a round black shape at the top of her foremast and a round black shape at the ends of her foreyard on the side or sides on which she is sweeping. By night, these shapes are replaced by all-round green lights in addition to her normal navigational lights. A vessel showing these shapes or lights is considered to be 'not under command' and therefore cannot get out of the way. All ships should give minesweepers a wide berth of at least half a mile.

Rule 5—Sailing Ships and Ships being Towed

These ships show red and green sidelights and a small white stern light. A sailing vessel may carry in addition at the top of her foremast two lights in a vertical line, clearly separated, the upper light red and the lower green.

By day a vessel being towed, if the length of the tow exceeds 600 feet, displays a black diamond shape where it can best be seen.

Rule 6—Portable Sidelights

If the weather is sufficiently bad to prevent the

placing of the red and green sidelights, they are to be kept ready for immediate display on the approach of another vessel in time to prevent a collision.

Rule 7—Lights for Small Vessels

Power-driven vessels less than 65 feet may carry lower powered lights than larger ships and may also vary the method in which the lights are fitted, including the use of a combined red and green lantern in lieu of sidelights. In addition, this Rule states that sailing vessels less than 40 feet may also use the combined red and green lantern, or have portable lights ready for exhibiting.

Small rowing boats, under oars or sail, need only show a small white light from an electric torch or lantern on being approached.

Rule 8—Pilot Vessels

Most pilot vessels nowadays are small power-driven vessels, and in this case they show a red light below a white light on the same mast, and green and red sidelights. The two lights on the mast must be visible all round the horizon.

In the case where a sailing ship is used as a pilot vessel the red light mentioned above is not carried.

All pilot vessels when on duty and under way show one or more flare-up lights at intervals not exceeding 10 minutes.

Rule 9—Fishing Vessels

All vessels engaged in fishing by day indicate their occupation by displaying two black cones, points together, one above the other, and if their tackle extends more than 500 feet they display an additional black cone, point upwards in the direction of the outlying gear. A fishing vessel less than 65 feet may substitute the two black cones for a basket.

By night, their lights indicate the type of fishing on which they are engaged. A vessel trawling shows a green light vertically above and separated from a white light, both visible all round the horizon. When under way, she shows her red and green sidelights and stern light, and may also show a white masthead steaming light, but this must always be abaft the green and white vertical lights.

All other vessels engaged in fishing show a red light in place of the green light, vertically above the white one, and if their gear extends more than 500 feet carry an additional all-round white light extended in the direction of the outlying gear.

To warn other vessels of impending danger, fishing vessels may also use a flare-up light or direct the beam of a searchlight in the direction of her gear.

Rule 10—Stern Lights

All large vessels must show a fixed stern light at night. In the case of small vessels this light may be portable.

Rule 11—Ships at Anchor

A vessel under 150 feet long at anchor shows one all-round white light high up in the bows.

A vessel over 150 feet in length at anchor shows one all-round white light high up in the bows and another similar light lower in the stern.

A ship at anchor during daytime indicates this by hoisting one black ball in the fore part of the vessel.

Rule 14—Sailing Vessels using Engines
A vessel under sail and also using her engines displays by day a black cone shape, point downwards, where it can best be seen.

Part C—Sound Signals in Fog or Restricted Visibility

Rules 15 and 16
These are the signals made by ships in fog to warn other ships of their presence. On power-driven vessels these signals are made by a whistle and on sailing ships by the use of a fog horn. A prolonged blast means one of about 5 seconds duration.

Power-driven vessels. When moving, one prolonged blast at 2-minute intervals.

When stopped, two prolonged blasts at 2-minute intervals.

Sailing Ships. On the starboard tack, one blast at 1-minute intervals.

On the port tack, two blasts at 1-minute intervals.

With the wind astern, three blasts at 1-minute intervals.

Ships at Anchor. A rapid ringing of the ship's bell for about 5 seconds every minute. If the length of the ship exceeds 350 feet, she must also sound a gong or other instrument in the stern for about 5 seconds every minute.

Hampered Vessels. Any ship that is hampered, i.e. a vessel not under command, a ship laying cable, a ship towing and a trawler trawling, has a special fog signal and this consists of one prolonged blast followed by two short blasts every minute. A vessel being towed, or, if more than one vessel is towed, then the last vessel of the tow, makes one prolonged blast followed by three short blasts at 1-minute intervals.

Note: See chapter on Boats and Boatwork for an explanation of tacking.

Part D—Steering and Sailing Rules

Rules 17—30 (including Part E and Part F)
This latter section of the Regulations for the Prevention of Collisions at Sea deals with the manner in which ships must manoeuvre when they approach each other. They are devised so that the vessel which has the greatest manoeuvrability is the one which keeps out of the way. For convenience let us summarise these rules in two sections: (a) rules for power-driven vessels and (b) rules for sailing ships. Remember that the words 'power-driven vessels' include all mechanically propelled craft from the largest liner to the smallest dinghy with an outboard engine.

The Preliminary to the Steering and Sailing Rules

This states that risk of collision can, when circumstances permit, be ascertained by watching the compass bearing of an approaching vessel. If the bearing does not appreciably change, then such risk should be deemed to exist. For instance, supposing you spot a ship in the distance coming towards you and using your compass with a special instrument fitted on the top called an 'Azimuth Mirror' you find that she is bearing, say, north 20 degrees east from you, and if after a few minutes you take another bearing of her and find the original bearing has not altered or has altered only slightly, then this means that both ships are heading for a common point and that, unless evading action is taken by one of the ships, collision will occur at this point.

Rules which apply to both Power-driven and Sailing Vessels

Any vessel which does not have to get out of the way of another must keep her course and speed, but at the same time she must keep a close watch on the other ship until danger of collision is over. If it happens that the ship which has to keep out of the way finds herself in difficulties arising from any unusual circumstances, then in this case the other ship must use discretion and, instead of keeping her course and speed, she may manoeuvre in any manner which will help to avoid collision (Rule 21).

Crossing ahead of another ship is to be avoided if possible. Any vessel overtaking must keep out of the way of the overtaken vessel until she is well clear of her (Rule 24). All vessels must carry the proper lights and signals and must maintain a good lookout (Rule 29). There must be no departure from these rules except in the case of immediate danger (Rule 27).

Rules for Power-driven Vessels

Power-driven vessels must keep out of the way of:

    (a)   Sailing vessels (Rule 20).
    (b)   Any vessel she is overtaking (Rule 24).
    (c)   Vessels or boats engaged in fishing (Rule 26).
    (d)   Any not-under-command or hampered vessels.

THE RULE OF THE ROAD AT SEA

When two power-driven vessels are meeting head on they must both alter course to starboard (Rule 18).

When the paths of two power-driven vessels are seen to be crossing, the vessel which has the other on her own starboard side keeps out of the way (Rule 19).

In narrow channels, rivers, etc., vessels must always keep to the right-hand side (Rule 25).

When a power-driven vessel in sight of another is making an alteration of course, according to these rules she should indicate her intentions by these signals on her whistle (Rule 28):

Altering to starboard—One short blast.
Altering to port—Two short blasts.
Engines going astern—Three short blasts.

A vessel which has to keep out of the way of another vessel may, if necessary, slacken her speed or stop or reverse (Rule 23).

Rules for Sailing Vessels

Sailing vessels must keep out of the way of:
  (a) Any vessel she is overtaking, including the rather rare case where she may be overtaking a power-driven vessel (Rule 24).
  (b) Vessels or boats engaged in fishing (Rule 26).
  (c) Any not-under-command or hampered vessels.

When two sailing vessels are approaching one another and are in danger of collision, one of them shall keep out of the way of the other as follows:
  (a) When each has the wind on different sides, the vessel which has the wind on the port side shall keep out of the way of the other.

(b)   When both have the wind on the same side, the vessel which is to windward shall keep out of the way of the vessel to leeward.

Note: For the purpose of this Rule the windward side shall be the side opposite to that on which the mainsail is set (Rule 17).

Part F—Miscellaneous

Rule 31—Distress Signals

Any vessel which is in distress and requires assistance from other vessels or from the shore must display or use the following, either together or separately:

(a)   A gun or other explosive signal fired at intervals of about 1 minute.

(b)   A continuous sounding on the ship's whistle or fog-horn.

(c)   Rockets or shells, throwing red stars, fired one at a time at short intervals.

(d)   The group S.O.S. in morse code by any signalling method.

(e)   The spoken word 'MAYDAY' sent by voice radio.

(f)   The International Code Signal Flags N.C.

(g)   A square flag having above or below it a ball, or anything resembling a ball.

(h)   Flames on the vessel (as from burning tar, oil barrel, etc.).

(i)   A rocket parachute flare or hand flare showing a red light.

(j)   A smoke signal giving off orange-coloured smoke.

(k)   Slowly and repeatedly raising and lowering outstretched arms to each side.

Note: Vessels in distress may use the radio-telegraph alarm signal, consisting of a series of 12 dashes in morse code, each of 4 seconds duration, transmitted in 1 minute with an interval of 1 second between each dash.

CHAPTER 5

TIDES AND BUOYAGE

Tides are caused chiefly by the attraction of the moon and partly by the attraction of the sun on the waters of the Earth. This is clearly shown by the fact that the highest high tides—*spring tides*—occur about the time of a full or new moon, i.e. at intervals of about 14 days, when the lunar and solar attractions act together. At *neap tides,* which occur roughly halfway between spring tides, the rise and fall of water is little more than half that of spring tides.

Rise and Fall

Since the Earth with its waters is rotating, every place as it comes under the influence of these external attractions has its waters gradually lifted to a maximum, then gradually dropped to a minimum. These effects of tide are most easily seen in a channel or estuary, where a rising tide is discernible as an incoming stream—a *flowing* or *flood tide*—and a falling tide is seen as an outgoing stream, or *ebb tide*.

Alternating high and low tides normally occur twice in each day—nearly $12\frac{1}{2}$ hours apart. This daily lag in time of about 50 minutes corresponds to the 24 hours 50 minutes average interval between successive passages of the moon across the meridian.

From what has been said, it might appear that the

tidal flow of water over the face of the Earth would be even and regular throughout. That this is not the case is due to a number of factors—some of which are highly complicated. The biggest single factor, however, is one which is fairly obvious—the shape of the various coastlines and the expanse of the waters separating them. Less obviously, the depth of seas plays an important part in contributing to the general irregularity.

In the open ocean, it is estimated that the rise and fall of the tides varies between 2 and 3 feet. Shallow seas, by diminishing the velocity, increase the height, and this may be further exaggerated by entry into converging channels or estuaries. Thus the difference between high and low water may vary from a few inches in the landlocked Mediterranean to 40 feet in the estuary of the Severn, or over 50 feet in the Bay of Fundy.

Nor is range of tide the only irregularity. The effect of shallow water and projecting land, giving rise to reflection and interference, is to set up *tidal currents* having little relationship to the true condition of tide. Such currents may give rise to double tides, as at Southampton, where the falling tide of the Channel driving through Spithead and the rising tide coming through the Solent each give high water.

From the foregoing it will be seen that there can be no fixed way of calculating tides and tidal currents, and the seaman falls back upon Nautical Almanacs and the Admiralty 'Pilots' for such vital information.

Around our coast are numerous buoys of various shapes and colours, so placed as to assist seamen to navigate their ships more safely in dangerous or narrow waters. These buoys at times may be forced away from their position by rough weather; therefore the seaman must only accept them as an aid to navigation, not as an infallible guide. There is a uniform system of buoyage in this country which is chiefly controlled and maintained by the Corporation of Trinity House.

The Main Stream of Flood Tide

It is important that the above term used in connection with buoyage should be understood because buoys have to be passed on one side when going with the main stream of flood and on the opposite side when going against it.

The main stream of flood tide is deemed to approach this country from the west, and on reaching a point off southern Ireland it splits into three streams. One of these streams follows the coast of western Ireland northwards until it meets a stream which travels up the Irish Sea, and the other stream flows up the English Channel until it reaches the Straits of Dover. The two former streams, now merged into one, pass around the north of Scotland and down the East Coast, meeting the English Channel stream at Dover. (Dover is the focal point for tides and on many charts the time of high water at a certain port is often referred to as so many hours before or after high water Dover.) When approaching a port from seaward the main stream of flood tide is always assumed to travel in this direction.

Buoys

Buoys are used to mark shipping channels, the edge of shoals or sandbanks, isolated dangers and wrecks. Any buoy may have a light on it and many buoys have bells or whistles attached which operate by the motion of the waves. The position of buoys and the character of their lights (if any) is shown on the charts.

Starboard-hand Buoys

These buoys are passed on the starboard or right-hand side of a vessel when proceeding in the direction of the main stream of flood or approaching a port from seaward. Starboard-hand buoys are conical in shape and painted black, or black and white chequers (see Fig. 31).

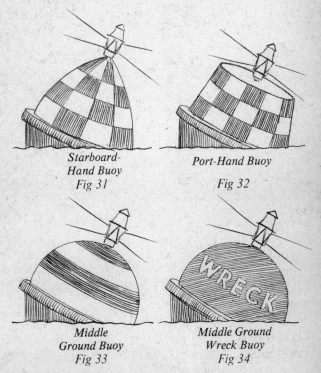

Starboard-
Hand Buoy
Fig 31

Port-Hand Buoy
Fig 32

Middle
Ground Buoy
Fig 33

Middle Ground
Wreck Buoy
Fig 34

Port-hand Buoys

These buoys are passed on the port or left-hand side of a vessel when proceeding in the direction of the main stream of flood or approaching a port from seaward. Port-hand buoys are can-shaped and painted red, or red and white chequers (see Fig. 32).

Middle Ground Buoys

These buoys are used to mark middle grounds, i.e. shoals in the middle of a channel, and they may be passed on either side. Middle ground buoys are spherical in shape and painted with either red and white or black and white horizontal stripes (see Fig. 33).

Note: Fig. 35 illustrates the use of each of the above buoys in a channel or estuary.

Wreck Buoys

These buoys mark the position of a wreck and are conical-, can- or spherical-shaped as ordinary buoys according to which side they may be passed. All wreck buoys are painted green and have the word 'WRECK' on them in white. When lit they show green flashes only (see Fig. 34).

Topmarks for Buoys

Many buoys are surmounted by a topmark to distinguish them from other buoys and to indicate to the seaman which is the inner or outer end of a shoal. Also, a number of buoys are named and have their names painted on them.

Light-vessels

These small vessels are moored in certain definite

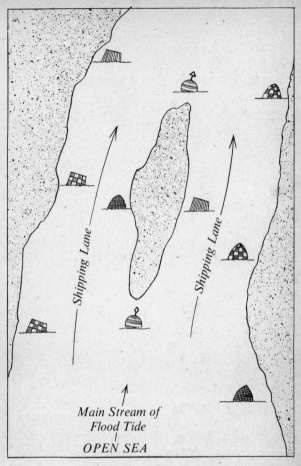

Shipping Lane

Shipping Lane

*Main Stream of
Flood Tide*

OPEN SEA

THE BUOYAGE SYSTEM

Fig 35

positions around the coast and serve as portable lighthouses. In fog they emit a characteristic fog signal and have proved themselves all round to be a very valuable aid to navigation. They are known by a name and this is painted in white letters on a red or black hull.

CHAPTER 6

FLAGS AND SIGNALS

The Flying of National Flags and Ensigns

A vessel flies the flag of the country and service which she represents. At sea this flag is generally flown from a small flagstaff placed high on the aftermost mast and 'colours' are shown from sunrise to sunset. In port the flag is flown lower down and usually on a small staff at the extreme stern of the vessel. In port or at anchor the flag is hoisted at 8 a.m. from the 25th March to the 20th September inclusive and at 9 a.m. from the 21st September to the 24th March inclusive. The flag is taken down at sunset. On large merchant ships and on almost all men-of-war this ceremony is accompanied by the bugle calls 'colours' and 'sunset'.

Note: Flags are not shown at sea when out of sight of land and other ships.

The Union Flag

Commonly called the Union Jack, this flag is a combination of the flags of the patron saints of England, Scotland and Ireland. England is represented by the cross of Saint George—a white flag with a red cross—Scotland by the cross of Saint Andrew—a blue flag with a white diagonal cross—and Ireland by the cross of Saint Patrick—a white flag with a red diagonal cross.

Wales has her own national flag which is the red Welsh dragon on a green and white background.

Ensigns

In our ensigns the Union flag is fitted into the top quarter of the flag nearest to the mast. The remaining three-quarters of these flags are plain red, white or blue, except the white ensign, which is actually the flag of Saint George with the Union Jack in the top left-hand corner. These flags are known as the red, white and blue ensigns respectively. They originated when the British fleet was divided into three squadrons, each squadron being represented by a colour, red then being the senior. In 1864 these colour squadrons were abolished and directions were issued, which are still in force, that the white ensign should be used by men-of-war, the blue ensign by vessels commanded by officers of the Royal Naval Reserve, and the red ensign by merchantmen and vessels of the fishing fleets.

Note: A merchant vessel may fly the blue ensign when a certain percentage of the officers and ratings are Royal Naval Reservists. The blue ensign with a crest in the fly, i.e. that part of the flag furthest from the mast, is often seen on special ships, e.g. Customs launches and some pilot vessels and Harbour Authority craft. A crest in the fly of a red or blue ensign is also that which is flown by vessels of the Dominions and Colonies.

Ensigns at Half Mast

This signifies either the death of a member of the crew, the death of some important national personage, or the death of an allied monarch or president, etc., and in each case it is a symbol of courtesy and mourning. In the event of the death of an important person in a merchant shipping company, it is common for all ships in that company to fly their ensigns at half mast. Further, for one year after, these ships may have a thin blue line painted around their hull as a symbol of mourning. Generally, ensigns do not remain at half mast for more than three days after death, or until burial.

When a flag is being hoisted to half mast it must first be struck to the top of the mast and then brought slowly down to half mast; similarly, before the flag is lowered at sunset it is first hoisted to the top of the mast.

Flags Upside Down
To allow this to happen is most unseamanlike. Contrary to popular belief this is not officially recognised as a maritime signal of distress.

Bow Flags
In port, ships which are entitled to fly the white ensign, i.e. men-of-war, may also fly a small Union flag from a jackstaff attached to the stem. Ships of the blue or red ensign may not fly the Union flag, but in place of this they are allowed a flag called the Pilot Jack. The Pilot Jack is a Union flag surrounded by a narrow white border. Some merchant ships in place of the Pilot flag prefer to fly their House Colours, i.e. the flag of the company which they represent, and this is permissible.

House Flags
As mentioned in the previous paragraph, a House Flag is the flag of a particular merchant company and most companies, whether or not they fly one of these at the bow, usually exhibit a large one from the mainmast. These vary considerably in colour and design.

Courtesy Flags

When a vessel is entering a foreign port she flies the flag of that country from her mainmast as a mark of respect. This flag is kept flying at the appropriate times for the duration of her stay in that country and is known as a Courtesy Flag.

Mail Pennants

A vessel carrying mail under contract to H.M. Post Office exhibits a white pennant with the words 'ROYAL MAIL' on it in red.

Saluting

Ships have a method of saluting each other at sea which is known as 'Dipping the Ensign'. Dipping the ensign is simply bringing the ensign to the position of half mast; the other vessel replies in the same manner and both flags are then hoisted up again. A red ensign always dips to a blue or a white, and the blue ensign dips to the white also. In vessels of the same fleet the junior ship always dips to the senior.

Signals

Communication at Sea

When vessels are out of sight of land they communicate with other vessels or with the shore by means of radiotelegraphy and/or radiotelephony.

When ships are in sight of one another or within sight of land the above methods may prove inconvenient or too expensive, in which case they signal visually. The most common form of visual signalling between ship and ship, or ship and shore, is the morse lamp, and this, of course, can be used by day or night. Another method of visual signalling during daytime is by semaphore; and finally there is the use of the International Code of Signals. Naval vessels have an additional method of daytime signalling which is exclusive to ships of war. This consists of a set of code flags each with different meanings comprising the Naval Code of Signals.

The Morse Code

There is no easy way of learning the morse code. To become proficient at receiving and sending you first have to memorise the morse alphabet thoroughly. The second thing is to increase your speed gradually, and this can only be achieved by continuous and regular practice. The speed used at sea in visual signalling varies between five and ten words a minute. In marine radiotelegraphy the speed averages about twenty-five words per minute.

When sending a message in morse, there should be a slight pause after each letter and a longer pause at the end of each word. The morse alphabet is so arranged that the letters which are most frequently used have the shortest symbols. No letter contains more than four symbols and numbers each have five symbols.

The Morse Alphabet

A · —	G — — ·	M — —	T —
B — · · ·	H · · · ·	N — ·	U · · —
C — · — ·	I · ·	O — — —	V · · · —
D — · ·	J · — — —	P · — — ·	W · — —
E ·	K — · —	Q — — · —	X — · · —
F · · — ·	L · — · ·	R · — ·	Y — · — —
		S · · ·	Z — — · ·

Morse Numerals

1	· — — — —	6	— · · · ·
2	· · — — —	7	— — · · ·
3	· · · — —	8	— — — · ·
4	· · · · —	9	— — — — ·
5	· · · · ·	0	— — — — —

Morse Procedure Signals. There are many procedure signs and signals in the morse code, but the actual use of some of them between visual signallers at sea is rare. This would apply more to merchant vessels than to men-of-war. In view of this, a number of the less used procedure signals have been omitted, but the following should be studied carefully as knowledge of their use is essential.

Sign	Morse Symbol	Meaning
AA AA AA etc.	· — · — · — etc.	A succession of double A's is known as the calling up sign and is used to attract the attention of a ship or shore station, etc.
TTTTTTTTTT	— — — — — — —	This is used by the receiving ship in answering the above calling up sign and is to be continued until the transmitting ship ceases to call.
DE	— · · ·	This is the 'from' sign used by the transmitting ship to precede its identity signal. This is repeated back by the receiving ship followed by its own identity signal.

T	—	This signal is made by the receiving ship at the end of each word to indicate that she has received it correctly.
EEEEE etc.	· · · · · · · ·	A succession of E's made by the transmitting ship indicates that she has made an error and wishes to erase the last word. This should be repeated back by the receiving ship, but in actual practice it is more often than not acknowledged simply by a T.
RPT	·—·—·—	This is the repeat signal. Used by the transmitting ship during the text of a message to indicate 'I repeat' or at the end to ask the receiving ship to repeat the message. Also used by the receiving ship when requesting a repetition. A correctly received repetition is then acknowledged with the symbol OK.
AR	·— ·—·	Used to indicate the end of a message.
R	·—·	Sent by the receiving ship to indicate that the message is received and understood.

Note: A bar over the letters composing a sign denotes the letters are to be made as one symbol.

A Model Message. A signal made by flashing light has four definite components as follows:

1. Call sign   AA AA AA, etc.
2. Identity   The two vessels identify them-
                      selves to each other (see meaning
                      of DE above).
3. The text of the message.
4. End of signal   AR.

The receiving ship answers the call sign by T TT T T, etc.; repeats the identity of the transmitting ship followed by her own identity; answers *each* word of the text with a T; and finally replies to AR with R, indicating that she has received the signal correctly.

Semaphore
This is a method of close range visual signalling by hand flags which has a limited application at sea today. It is particularly useful between ships in harbour, between two ships travelling close together in the same direction and as intercommunication between ships in convoy.

Procedure. The vessel intending to transmit by sema-phore hoists the International Code Signal K1 ('I wish to communicate with you by semaphore'). The receiving ship then hoists the answering pennant at the dip, i.e. about halfway up to show that the Signal K1 has been observed, and when she is ready to receive the message the answering pennant will be hoisted close up (see Fig. 36).

Any number which occurs in the message must be spelt out in words. When ships are close together the

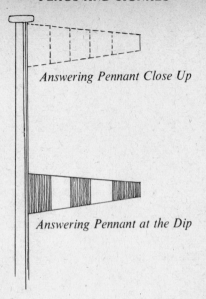

Answering Pennant Close Up

Answering Pennant at the Dip

Fig. 36

International Code Signal K1 and the answering pennant need not be used, but if not, the attention sign and answering sign (see Fig. 37) are used instead.

Special Signs. These are not so detailed as in morse and are used as follows:

1. Attention   Waving the flags from the position U to N until attention is attracted and acknowledged by the answering sign C.
2. Answering   Sign C.
3. Break Sign   The flags at rest in front of the legs. This precedes a message and follows each word of text.

4. Erase Sign   A succession of E's indicates
                      that an error has been made.
                      The sender continues making
                      this signal until answered by a
                      C, when he then transmits the
                      last word correctly.
5. Ending Sign   The same as in morse, namely
                      AR.

Note: If the sender does not observe the answering
sign C at the end of a word, he should repeat the
word until it is answered in such manner.

Semaphore Signalling. When sending make sure
that your background is such that the receiving
ship can see your signals to the best advantage.
The arm, wrist and flag should form one straight
line, and care must be taken to form the angles
correctly. The body should be kept upright and the
legs together. The break sign is not used at the end
of individual letters comprising a word, but when
double letters occur, e.g. O-F-F-I-C-E-R, the flags
are brought to the break position after the first
double letter and then moved to the second letter
without pausing. In moving from one letter to the
next the arms should be kept straight and swung
through a vertical plane.

Learning semaphore will be simplified if you
observe that the alphabet is divided into three
'circles' and some irregular letters. Master one
circle at a time until you can transmit or receive
rapidly any letter in that circle. The three circles
are (a) A to G, (b) H to N (omitting J) and (c) O
to S. The remainder, including J, are termed
irregular letters.

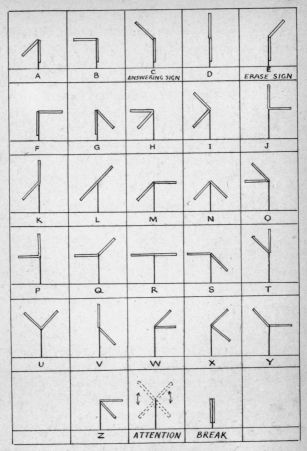

THE SEMAPHORE ALPHABET

Fig 37

Phonetic Tables

When signals are sent by voice either by radio-telephony or loud-hailer and it is required to spell out words or figures, the following code words are used for the individual letters of the alphabet:

Letter	Code Word	Pronounced (syllables emphasised are in capitals
A	Alfa	*AL*fah
B	Bravo	*BRAH* voh
C	Charlie	*CHAR* lee
D	Delta	*DELL* tah
E	Echo	*ECK* oh
F	Foxtrot	*FOKS* trot
G	Golf	Golf
H	Hotel	Hoh *TELL*
I	India	*IN* dee ah
J	Juliet	*JEW* le *ETT*
K	Kilo	*KEY* loh
L	Lima	*LEE* mah
M	Mike	Mike
N	November	No *VEM* ber
O	Oscar	*OSS* cah
P	Papa	Pah *PAH*
Q	Quebec	Keh *BECK*
R	Romeo	*ROW* me oh
S	Sierra	See *AIR* rah
T	Tanko	*TANG* go
U	Uniform	*YOU* nee form
V	Victor	*VIK* tah
W	Whiskey	*WISS* key
X	X-ray	*ECKS* ray
Y	Yankee	*YANG* key
Z	Zulu	*ZOO* loo

The International Code of Signals
Because of language difficulties, a code of signals for the use of mariners has always been used. The book is carried by all seagoing ships and is printed in nine different laguages: English, French, German, Italian, Spanish, Japanese, Norwegian, and more recently in Russian and Greek.

The International Code of Signals was revised in 1969 to achieve simplicity and reduce the volume of the Code, which prior to 1969 was contained in two books. The Code is now suitable for transmission by all types of communication and enables ships to exchange information with each other no matter what their nationality may be. Each signal in the revised Code has a complete meaning, and the book is arranged in a code and de-code system which is easy to follow. It caters mainly for distress, and safety of ships and persons.

The Code Flags. A complete set of International Code Flags consists of 26 alphabetical flags, 10 numeral pendants, 3 substitutes and the answering pendants (see Fig. 38).

A signal may consist of one, two or three flags, supplemented if necessary by numeral pendants which vary the basic signal.

Single-letter Signals. When flown singly, each letter of the alphabet has a meaning of special significance:

A   I have a diver down.
*B   I am taking in, or discharging, or carrying dangerous goods.
C   Yes (affirmative).

*D   Keep clear of me, I am manoeuvring with difficulty.

*E   I am altering my course to starboard.

 F   I am disabled. Communicate with me.

 G   I require a pilot.

*H   I have a pilot on board.

*I   I am altering my course to port.

 J   I am on fire and have a dangerous cargo on board, keep well clear of me.

 K   I wish to communicate with you.

 L   You should stop your vessel instantly.

 M   My vessel is stopped and making no way through the water.

 N   No (negative).

 O   Man overboard.

 P   At sea: it may be used by fishing vessels to mean 'My nets have come fast upon an obstruction'. In harbour: all persons should report on board as the vessel is about to proceed to sea.

 Q   My vessel is 'healthy' and I request free practique.

*S   My engines are going astern.

*T   Keep clear of me; I am engaged in pair trawling.

 U   You are running into danger.

 V   I require assistance.

 W   I require medical assistance.

 X   Stop carrying out your intentions and watch for my signals.

 Y   I am dragging my anchor.

 Z   I require a tug. When made by fishing vessels operating in close proximity on the fishing grounds it means 'I am shooting nets'.

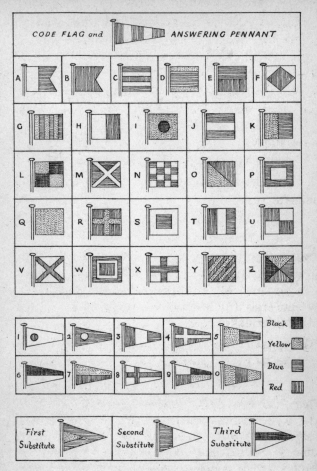

CODE FLAG and ANSWERING PENNANT

A B C D E F
G H I J K
L M N O P
Q R S T U
V W X Y Z

1 2 3 4 5
6 7 8 9 0

Black
Yellow
Blue
Red

First Substitute
Second Substitute
Third Substitute

Fig 38

Note: Signals of letters marked * when made by sound may only be made in compliance with the requirements of the International Regulations for the Prevention of Collisions at Sea, Rules 15 and 28.

Two-letter Signals. Signals containing two-letter groups are from the General Section of the Code and refer mainly to the safety of navigation and persons, for example:

> SQ   You should stop, or heave to.

Two-letter groups can be supplemented by a numeral, thus:

> SQ 2 You should stop, or heave to: I am going to send a boat.

Three-letter Signals. Signals containing three-letter groups are from the medical section and all begin with the letter 'M'. The groups may be supplemented by numerals from tables of complements to give added information, e.g.:

> MGH   Patient has severe burn ...
> MGH 33 Patient has severe burn ... front of leg.

Four- and Five-letter Signals. Signals consisting of four letters are allocated to ships for identification purposes. Thus the radio call sign of a ship is the same as her signal letters; the first or the first and second letters indicate the nationality of the ship. British ships' signal letters begin with either G or M.

The signal letters and radio call signs of aircraft are made up of five-letter groups.

International Code—Flag Signalling Procedure. A vessel wishing to communicate with a particular ship should hoist the ship's signal letters superior to the signal. If no identity signal is hoisted, it will be understood that the signal is addressed to all ships within signalling distance.

The ship addressed will hoist the answering pendant at the dip on observing the hoist and close up when it is understood. This is repeated for as many signal groups as the transmitting ship wishes to send and is always answered in the same manner by the receiving ship. At the end of the message, the transmitting ship hoists the answering pendant singly to indicate that the signal is completed, and the receiving ship answers this in a similar manner to all other hoists.

The Use of Substitutes. Most seagoing vessels carry at least two sets of code flags, but in the case where only one set is carried it would be impossible without the use of substitutes to signal the group say GB*TT*.

First Substitute	always repeats the first or uppermost flag in the hoist.
Second Substitute	always repeats the second flag from the top of the hoist.
Third Substitute	always repeats the third flag from the top of the hoist.

The group GBTT would now read:

1. G
2. B
3. T
4. Third substitute.

It will be noticed from the above example that the third substitute repeats the third flag from the top of the hoist, namely (T).

Life-saving Signals

The following signals are used by the Life-saving Services to assist and give direction and information to seamen in distress.

1. Landing signals for the guidance of small boats with crews or persons in distress:

Signal	*Signification*
By day: Vertical motion of a white flag or of the arms. By night: Vertical motion of a white light or flare	This is the best place to land.

or

By day or night: Firing of a green star signal

or

The letter K made by light or sound-signal apparatus.

By day: Horizontal motion of a white flag or arms. By night: Horizontal motion of a white flag or flare	Landing here is dangerous.

or

By day or night: Firing of red star signal

or

The letter S made by light or sound-signal apparatus.

By day: Horizontal motion of a white flag, followed by the placing of the	Landing here is highly dangerous. A more favourable location for

white flag in the ground and carrying another white flag in the direction to be indicated.

By night: Horizontal motion of a white flare or light, followed by the placing of a white light or flare on the ground and carrying another white light or flare in the direction to be indicated

or

By day or night: Firing of a red star signal vertically and a white star signal in the direction towards the better landing place

or

Signalling the Code letter S, followed by the Code letter R or L (right or left) indicating the direction of approach.

landing is in the direction indicated.

2. Signals to be employed in connection with the use of shore life-saving apparatus:

Signal	*Signification*
By day: Vertical motion of a white flag or of the arms. By night: Vertical motion of a white light or flare.	In general—affirmative. Specifically—rocket line is held. Tail block is made fast. Hawser is made fast. Man is on the Breeches

Buoy.
Haul away.

By day: Horizontal motion of a white flag or arms. By night: Horizontal motion of a white light or flare.	In general—negative. Specifically — slack away, avast hauling.

3. Replies from life-saving stations or maritime rescue units to distress signals made by a ship or person:

Signal	*Signification*
By day: Orange smoke signal *or* Combined light and sound signal (thunder-light) consisting of 3 single signals fired at intervals of 1 minute. By night: White star rocket consisting of 3 single signals at intervals of 1 minute.	You are seen—assistance will be given as soon as possible.

CHAPTER 7

ANCHORS AND CABLES

Anchors are made of cast steel, forged open hearth ingot steel, or forged wrought iron. All anchors are hammered and drop tested for flaws; they are also annealed and stamped 'Annealed Steel'.

A ship carries one anchor on either side of the bows, these being called bower anchors. She also carries a spare bower anchor situated conveniently on the foredeck.

On the deck in the stern of the ship is an anchor called a stream anchor, which is about one-third the weight of a bower anchor. A stream anchor is only used when stern moorings are required. On most vessels the stream anchor is used on the end of a stout wire hawser, but some vessels which trade to ports where stern moorings are often required are fitted with a windlass, a length of chain cable and a hawse pipe to permanently house the anchor. Hawse pipes are large steel pipes through which the cable runs and in which the shank of a stockless anchor is housed when not in use. The weight of a bower anchor of a ship of 8000 tons is about $3\frac{1}{2}$ tons.

Types of Anchors

Admiralty Pattern and Stockless Anchors

There are several types of anchors, but the two in

common use on board ship are (i) the Admiralty
pattern anchor and (ii) the Stockless anchor (see
Figs. 39 and 40).

Bower anchors are invariably of the stockless
types, the advantage being the greater ease with

ADMIRALTY PATTERN

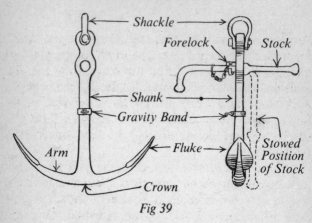

Fig 39

STOCKLESS

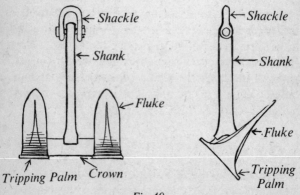

Fig 40

which they can be handled and stowed in the hawse pipes. The stockless anchor is constructed so that the flukes will turn to an angle of 45 degrees on each side of the shank.

The Kedge Anchor

A light anchor, generally of Admiralty pattern, used for kedging a ship from place to place; that is, the anchor is carried out to a distance from the ship and dropped. The ship is then pulled up to it by means of windlass or winches. It is the smallest anchor on board.

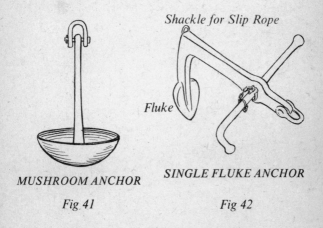

Shackle for Slip Rope

Fluke

MUSHROOM ANCHOR

SINGLE FLUKE ANCHOR

Fig. 41

Fig 42

The Mushroom Anchor

This is generally used for mooring light-vessels around our coasts. Two mushroom anchors are used for this purpose, the cables of each being joined together just under the water by a large swivel (see Fig. 41).

The Single Fluke Anchor

Used as a permanent mooring anchor for buoys and beacons, it is lowered to the bottom by means of a slip rope rove through a shackle in the crown. To prevent these buoys or beacons from shifting position with a change of wind or tide they often have three of these anchors spread out on the sea bed with the ends of their cables and the cable from the buoy attached to a swivel (see Fig. 42).

The Screw Mooring Anchor

This is sometimes used in place of a single fluke anchor depending on the nature of the sea bed. Screw moorings are only used when the sea bed is very soft (see Fig. 43).

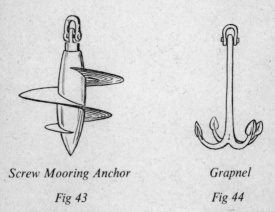

Screw Mooring Anchor   Grapnel

Fig 43   Fig 44

The Grapnel

This is sometimes used as an anchor for small boats. It is reminiscent of sailing ship days when grappling irons were used to close vessels together for hand to hand fighting (see Fig. 44).

The Sea Anchor

This is part of the equipment carried in a ship's lifeboat and is described in greater detail in Chapter 11. It is not, strictly speaking, an anchor at all, being simply a canvas bag attached to a line which is allowed to drift ahead of a boat in rough weather, enabling her to keep head to wind and sea and lessening her 'lee drift', i.e. her drifting away from the wind (see Fig. 45).

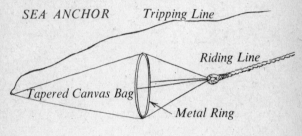

Fig 45

Anchor Cables

The chain cable, which is shackled to the end of each bower anchor, has studs fitted in the links which strengthen the chain and prevent it from kinking. This cable is supplied to vessels in lengths of 15 fathoms, 1 fathom equalling 6 feet, and these lengths are joined together by shackles. A 15-fathom length of cable is referred to by seamen as a 'shackle of cable'.

On almost all modern ships these joining shackles take the form of patent links, and unless a patent link is closely inspected it is almost indistinguishable from an ordinary link. These links can be dismantled into two halves by withdrawing a pin. Chain cable is measured by the diameter of the links and on a vessel of 8000 tons it would be about $2\frac{1}{4}$ inches. The same vessel would be supplied with about 8/10 shackles of cable for each bower anchor (see Figs. 46a and 46b).

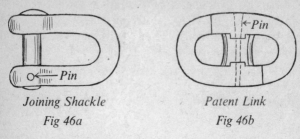

Joining Shackle   *Patent Link*

Fig 46a   *Fig 46b*

Marking of Shackles

The lengths of cable are marked as follows:

At the first shackle abaft the anchor (15 fathoms) there is a piece of seizing wire on the studs of the links immediately in front of and behind the patent link. At the second shackle (30 fathoms), there is a piece of seizing wire on the studs of the second links in front of and behind the patent link, and so on (see Fig. 46c).

Anchor Cable Marked at the 2nd Shackle

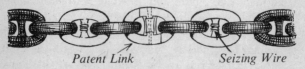

Patent Link   *Seizing Wire*

Fig. 46c

To enable the shackles to be still more easily identified each patent link and all the links which are dressed with seizing wire are painted white. Seizing wire is small seven-strand soft steel wire.

The Passage of the Cable from the Water to the Chain Locker

The cable leads up through the *Hawse Pipes,* or large tubes in either bow, over *Compressors* which are used to grip the cable and hold it in position when the vessel is at sea, and thence to the *Windlass.* The windlass is powered by steam or electricity and rotates two drums which are specially shaped to take the cables; these drums are known as *Gypsies.* The

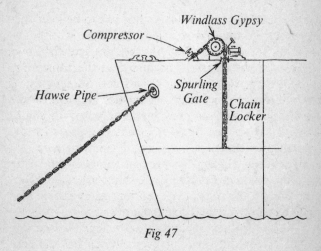

Fig 47

cable then drops vertically downwards from the gypsies through the *Spurling Gates* to the *Chain Locker* below. The chain locker end of the cable is always secured to the bottom of the locker by means of either a chain lashing or a special slip link (see Fig. 47).

In the Royal Navy and on some large merchant ships the cables are handled by *Capstans.* With a capstan the shaft and drum revolve vertically instead of horizontally. In this case the gypsies are replaced by drums which revolve flat on the deck and are known as *Cable Holders*. Another difference, in name only this time, is that the hole or tube from the deck which leads to the chain locker is termed the *Navel Pipe* instead of the spurling gate. Both gypsies and cable holders are controlled by powerful hand brakes.

Anchoring

While a ship is at sea the anchor has to be kept very securely in the hawse pipe, and this is done by making sure that the hand brakes are screwed down tightly on the gypsies and also that the cable compressors are tight around the cables. Sometimes, as an additional precaution, the cables are lashed with small chain or large claw hooks attached to chains (known as anchor dogs or devil's claws) which are placed over the cables. At sea the spurling gates are plugged and covered to prevent the entry of water into the chain locker. On some ships, instead of plugs and covers, the tops of the spurling gates are plugged with cotton waste and cemented over.

The first job in anchoring is to clear the spurling gates, remove the lashings from the cables and ease back the compressors. This would be done about an hour before the anticipated time of anchoring, and shortly after this an officer and a small party of men would assemble on the forecastle head; as the vessel approached her anchorage, they would place the gypsy of the anchor they intend using in gear and lower the anchor to within a few feet of the water's edge. When the anchor is in this position the windlass is stopped, the handbrake is placed on and the gypsy taken out of gear.

The anchor is now all ready for dropping at the word of command from the bridge. Before this final act, the ship is brought head to wind or tide and stopped. The engines are put astern and as soon as the ship has sternway, i.e. commences to move astern, the anchor is let go by releasing the windlass brake.

As each marked shackle passes over the gypsy, the number of shackles out is signalled to the bridge by strokes on the ship's bell which usually hangs just behind the windlass. These strokes must always be made singly, never as double rings in the manner of time bells. The officer on the forecastle head also signals to the bridge the direction in which the cable is leading by indicating this with his arm. This greatly assists the people on the bridge of the ship, especially in the case where the cable is leading astern due to the vessel not having sufficient sternway on when the anchor was dropped. At night or in fog, anchoring a ship is a little more difficult, and in this case communication between bridge and forecastle head is usually maintained by telephone.

When the required amount of cable is out— usually a length about three or four times the depth of water—the brake is screwed up. When the cable becomes taut and then slackens off again, indicating that the anchor is holding, the ship is then said to be 'Brought up'.

If through weather conditions it is necessary to let go another anchor, the engines are placed ahead and the vessel is given a sheer away from the first anchor before letting go the second. If a vessel is anchored in a tideway in this manner, it will be necessary to pick one anchor up before the turn of each tide to prevent the cables from crossing.

A vessel at anchor should always have her main engines available for immediate use to prevent the ship from becoming helpless in the event of a sudden worsening of the weather, or any unusual accidents or emergencies.

Note: It has been stated that the anchor is lowered almost to the water's edge before dropping and this is general practice, but in an emergency it may be dropped from the hawse pipe.

Weighing Anchor

The term weighing the anchor simply means heaving it in, and this is done by engaging the gears of the gypsy, releasing the handbrake and starting the windlass. Each shackle coming in is signalled to the bridge as before, and if the sea bed is known to be mud or clay, etc., then a hose is played on the cable as it comes up the hawse pipe. The officer on the forecastle head signals as before the direction in which the cable is leading, and as soon as the cable leads 'up and down' this means the anchor is broken out of the ground—a fact which is immediately communicated to the bridge by a short rapid ringing of the ship's bell. The shank of the anchor is hove (drawn) up into the hawse pipe and secured, the spurling gate is plugged and covered, and the vessel is then ready for sea.

Day Mark for a Vessel at Anchor

An internationally adopted signal for a ship at anchor by day is that she shall display in the fore part of the vessel where it can best be seen, one black ball or shape at least 2 feet in diameter. For night-time signal, see Chapter 4.

CHAPTER 8

MOORING AND BERTHING

Mooring

If a vessel is anchored as described in the last chapter and also happens to be in a tideway, she will obviously need a lot of room to swing around at the change of the tide. Whenever it is desired that she should occupy as little room as possible, the process of mooring is adopted.

Mooring is the art of placing a ship midway between two anchors so that on the flood tide she rides to one anchor and on the ebb tide to the other, and at the turn of the tide she swings around in practically her own length without fouling her cables.

One disadvantage of being moored is that in the event of a strong wind springing up across the line of mooring the anchors would be placed in their least advantageous position and the vessel may drag them along the bottom. Another disadvantage is that should bad weather come from a direction in line with the moorings the second anchor would be astern and of no use in helping to hold the ship. Mooring, therefore, is usually only adopted when weather conditions are fine and stable, and, as previously mentioned, when it is desirous that the ship should occupy as little room as possible.

There are two methods of mooring a ship, the first and most common being known as a standing or ordinary moor, and the second as a running moor.

Making a Standing Moor

The anchorage is approached head to tide and the
vessel brought at dead slow speed to a point about a
ship's length *ahead* of where she is eventually to be
moored. The engines are stopped, and as soon as she
starts to move astern with the tide the port anchor is
let go. The cable is slacked away and gradually
checked until there are just over six shackles of cable
out. When she is 'brought up' on the port anchor the

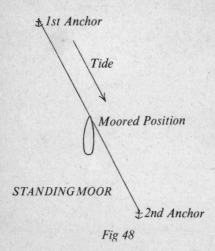

Fig 48

starboard anchor is let go underfoot. Then, using the
engines to ease the strain, the port cable is hove in
and the starboard one slacked out until there are
about three shackles of cable on each anchor (see
Fig. 48).

Making a Running Moor

The anchorage is again approached head to tide, but
in this case the vessel is brought to a point about a

ship's length *astern* of where she is to be moored. Here the port anchor is let go, with the ship still steaming dead slow ahead, and the cable is payed out, using the engines when necessary to check her, until there are just over six shackles out. The engines are stopped, and as soon as the ship starts to drop astern with the tide the starboard anchor is let go. The port cable is now hove in and the starboard one slacked out until there are about three shackles on each anchor (see Fig. 49).

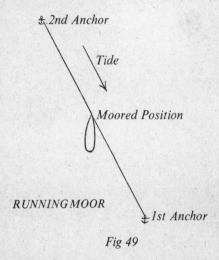

Fig 49

Note: It has been assumed above that an average ship of, say, 450 feet in length is being moored in a depth of 10 to 15 fathoms of water.

Unmooring
The cable which the ship is riding to at the time is 'veered', i.e. slacked out, until it is possible to weigh

the other anchor. The riding anchor is then weighed in the normal manner.

A Few Hints on Mooring

In cases where there is a weak tide and a stronger wind, then the ship is brought head to wind before mooring. Sometimes the tide may run stronger in one particular direction or the wind may prevail from a certain quarter, and in this case it is advisable to allow a greater length of cable in the direction from which the strongest tide or wind is anticipated. Just before the tide turns, it is recommended to use the steering wheel to give the vessel a sheer in the direction she is required to swing after the tide changes. This may save hours of work later in the event of the vessel swinging the wrong way and getting the anchor cables crossed.

Foul Hawse

This is the term used when a vessel's cables have become crossed. Clearing foul hawse can be a very tricky operation and it is always performed under the supervision of an experienced officer. The actual method employed, of which there are several, depends upon the circumstances and the personal efficiency of the officer concerned.

The Use of the Stream Anchor

As stated before, if a vessel is trading to a port where stream anchors are frequently used, she is usually fitted with a windlass arrangement similar to that in the bows for handling her stream anchor. The case occasionally arises where a vessel not so fitted is required to put out stern moorings, and in this event the stream anchor is handled and brought into position by using the nearest derrick or crane. A stout wire rope is shackled to the anchor, the rope is then flaked on deck and the end secured to a pair of bitts (see **Berthing**). With the anchor held in position a strong fibre rope lashing is placed on, and the runner from the derrick or crane then removed. At the word of command for the stream anchor to be let go, all persons stand well clear of the wire flaked on the deck and one man releases the anchor by severing the fibre rope lashing.

The stream anchor being used from the stern of a ship is not for the purpose of anchoring. Its function is to prevent a vessel from swinging or sheering about in narrow waters, i.e. rivers, inlets, etc., where there is no tide. Also, it is sometimes used to assist in bringing a vessel alongside a quay or jetty when no tugs are available.

Berthing

When a vessel is approaching or about to leave a quayside or berth, all the available engine room hands assemble in the engine room and take up stations in readiness to carry out the 'ahead' or 'astern' engine movements as ordered from the bridge. The deck department receives the order to 'stand by fore and aft'. This means that the bosn details the deck ratings into two parties, one of which takes up station in the bows and the other in the stern, each party being under the supervision and direction of an officer or officers. The officer in charge of the bow party is usually the chief or first officer, while the second officer takes charge at the stern. On the bridge the Captain is in charge with the third officer as his assistant. When a pilot is on board he acts in an advisory capacity only, the Captain of the ship being responsible at all times for the navigation and safe handling of his ship.

Preparations for Going Alongside

The manner in which a ship approaches a quayside to 'tie up' depends on the state of the tide and the force and direction of the wind, so let us assume for the purpose of illustration that perfect weather conditions prevail, i.e. no wind or tide.

The pilot will usually advise both bow and stern parties which side of the vessel is going to be secured to the quay, i.e. port or starboard. Once this is known all the ropes can be flaked down on deck on that side ready for running out to the shore.

The windlass in the bow and the poop windlass in the stern are tested to make sure they are running smoothly. The method of communication between the bridge and the bow, stern and engine room, i.e. telephone or mechanical telegraph, is tested, and all the ship's clocks and watches are set at the same time. The time factor is important because each operation and each movement of the engines is recorded in the log books of both the deck and engine departments, and there must be no discrepancies in time. This would particularly apply in the event of an accident which is investigated by an outside authority.

When a ship is berthing she should never be in direct contact with the quayside, and to keep her off a bit and prevent damage to both the ship and the quay the Harbour Authorities sometimes provide timber floats which are moored alongside. These are known as 'catamarans'. Where catamarans are not provided the ship hangs a number of fenders over her side. Fenders are either bundles of timber lashed together or cork-filled rope bags, these serving the same purpose as catamarans.

A ship's mooring ropes or hawsers are heavy to handle and cannot therefore be passed directly to the shore, but this is overcome by sending a light line ashore first with the hawser attached to it by a bowline. These light lines, known as 'heaving lines', are weighted at one end and are thrown ashore in the manner of a lasso, several of them being kept handy at each end of the ship. Harbour Authorities also keep heaving lines in readiness on the quayside; these are specially useful when a vessel is approaching a berth and there is a strong offshore wind.

Securing Alongside

A ship usually approaches her berth with her bows canted towards the quayside in order to keep her propeller well clear of any obstructions; therefore, the first hawser to be placed out is generally a head rope (see Fig. 50). This is usually followed by a stern rope, and these two ropes are then used to heave the ship in broadside to the quay. With the ship alongside, backsprings are placed out, followed by breast ropes, and finally two or three more head and stern ropes are secured.

The head, stern and breast ropes are generally 8–12 inch fibre ropes, and the backsprings 3–4 inch flexible steel ropes. In some ports where there is a big rise and fall of tide, or where the berth is exposed to an ocean swell, 'coir' backsprings are used (see Chapter 2).

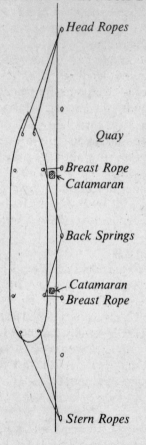

Head Ropes

Quay

Breast Rope
Catamaran

Back Springs

Catamaran
Breast Rope

Stern Ropes

Fig 50

Breast ropes are used to prevent the ship from surging away from the quayside, and if the ship is berthed in a tideway, or if she is loading or discharging cargo, then these ropes will need regular attention.

The first party to finish berthing—usually the bow party—places the gangway out from the ship in position. One end of this gangway is secured inboard and the other end, which is usually fitted with wheels or rollers, is allowed to rest on the quay.

Belaying a Rope
To secure the end of a rope in a fixed position or to 'belay' it, or 'make fast' (to use the correct nautical expression), is obviously essential in the case of mooring ropes. Small ropes are belayed to 'cleats' (see Fig. 51), but larger ropes are belayed to 'bitts' or 'bollards' (see Fig. 52). These bitts or bollards are simply twin steel posts set in the deck close to the rotating drum of the windlass or capstan.

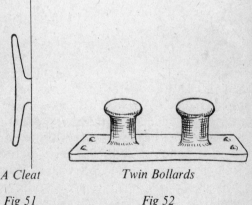

A Cleat   *Twin Bollards*

Fig 51   *Fig 52*

Imagine a heavy hawser made fast to a bollard on the shore, and leading back to the ship and being hove tightly on the drum of the windlass. Because of the weight in the 'bight' of rope leading from the ship, it would be impossible to transfer the rope from the drum to the bitts by hand. The rope would simply take charge and slack off again. This is overcome by the use of a stopper. A stopper is a short length of about $2\frac{1}{2}$-inch rope made fast to a ringbolt in the deck near the bitts. When the hawser is hove tight the order is given to 'stopper off', and this is done by passing the stopper round the hawser and making a half hitch against the lay, then passing several turns around the rope with the lay (see Fig. 53).

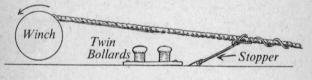

STOPPERING OFF

Fig 53

When this is done the order is given to 'ease to the stopper' and the hawser is gently eased from the drum of the windlass until the stopper is taking all the weight. The hawser is taken to the bitts and belayed in a figure-of-eight fashion (see Fig. 54). About three turns is enough for fibre rope, but twice this number of turns is used in the case of steel rope.

HAWSER BELAYED TO TWIN BOLLARDS

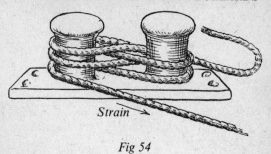

Strain →

Fig 54

The principle in stoppering off a steel rope is the same as for a fibre rope, the only difference being that a length of small chain is used as a stopper, and in this case the half hitch is made with the lay and the turns against the lay.

CHAPTER 9

CARGO WORK

The purpose of a merchant ship is to carry cargo, and the primary duty of a ship's crew is to work as a team to ensure that the cargo is carefully handled in order to avoid damage, to see that it is properly and securely stowed in the vessel's holds so that the ship will be stable and seaworthy, and virtually to nurse the cargo to its destination and deliver it in good condition.

Let us consider, in the main, cargo work as applied to the general cargo ship, of which the bulk of our fleet is composed.

Cargo Hatchways and Holds

Hatchways (Fig. 55)
A hatchway, literally speaking, is simply a large opening in the deck. This opening necessitates the severing of many of the transverse beams which support the deck above them, so to restore this lost strength a vertical steel wall about 3 feet high called a *Hatch Coaming* is erected around the hatchway, and the deck is supported underneath by additional longitudinal girders. To close the hatchway to the elements and to make the vessel seaworthy after loading or discharging cargo *Portable Beams* are used which fit into slots on the inside of the hatch coaming. The

beams are placed transversely, the tops of them being flanged to take a number of wooden *Hatchboards* which slide across them and rest fore and aft. When the beams and hatchboards are in place, a flat surface is presented across the top of the hatch coaming and this is covered over with three canvas tarpaulins, the oldest tarpaulin being placed on top. These tarpaulins are secured by the process of *Battening Down,* i.e. the edges are turned inwards and jammed hard up against the hatch coamings by means of steel battens and wooden wedges (see Fig. 56).

The above method of closing hatches with beams and hatchboards, though not obsolete, is not used in

A CARGO HATCHWAY

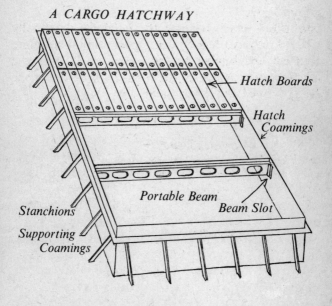

Fig 55

new construction ships. The beams and hatchboards are being superseded by patent hatch covers of large hinged lids made of steel which lift off in one piece, or self-stowing sectional slab hatches which roll on wheels and fold up like a concertina. These hatch covers are opened and closed by a power-operated mechanism which enables the hatches to be sealed or opened up in very quick time compared with the time-consuming, and sometimes dangerous, handling of hatchboards and beams. Ships fitted with wooden hatch covers are, by the New Load Line Regulations, not allowed to load as deeply as ships fitted with the patent steel hatch covers.

Cargo Holds

The cargo space beneath the hatchway is usually divided into two sections, the upper section being the smallest and known as the 'tween deck', and the lower section which is the main bulk of the space being termed the 'lower hold' (see Chapter 1). The

BATTENING DOWN A HATCH

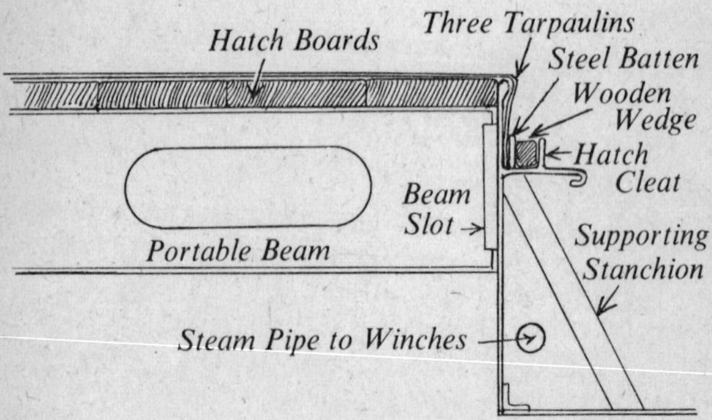

Fig 56

floor of the lower hold which lies directly beneath the hatchway is referred to as the 'square of the hatch'. This part of the floor is always covered with $2\frac{1}{2}$- to 3-inch planking, which is known as the 'lower hold ceiling'. The purpose of this ceiling is to protect the double bottom tanks from any heavy cargo which may be accidently dropped or mishandled in the hatchway.

Sweating and the Use of 'Dunnage'

When travelling on a crowded bus or train, it will be noticed that moisture tends to form on the inside of the windows. The only way to prevent this is by some system of ventilation. Exactly the same thing happens on a ship. The inside of a ship, i.e. the cargo holds, is invariably warmer than the outside air and water, so condensation or sweat forms on the inside. As in the case of the bus or train, this can be greatly reduced by efficient ventilation, but on a ship carrying thousands of tons of cargo, probably loaded in a hot climate, sweating cannot be entirely eliminated. The nature of the cargo itself contributes greatly to the amount of condensation; for instance, with a cargo of scrap iron this would be negligible, but with a cargo of, say, cocoa beans there could be an enormous amount of sweating.

Sweat forming on the sides of the ship will obviously run down to the floor of the hold, but this is prevented from damaging the lower tier of cargo by pieces of wood which are laid criss-cross over all the steel parts of the lower hold. These pieces of wood are termed *Dunnage Wood,* and on the bottom of the hold the first tier of dunnage is laid athwartships and on top of this are pieces laid fore and aft. The reason for laying the first tier arthwartships is that a ship always rolls from side to side more than she pitches, thus giving the water more chance of finding its way unobstructed to the sides of the ship and thence to the *Bilges*. The bilge is simply a shallow well or trough where moisture can collect and be pumped out by a valve operated in the engine room.

Note: The lower hold ceiling (mentioned in the paragraph on Cargo Holds) forms what is known as permanent dunnage, and no further dunnage wood is needed on top of this.

On the side framing of the ship are *Portable Wooden Side Battens*. These are boards about 6 inches broad and 2 inches thick, spaced about 9 inches apart and usually arranged horizontally. Although they are called portable side battens they form, together with the ceiling, the permanent dunnage of the ship. The only time they are removed is for repair, or when a bulk cargo of coal, scrap iron or the like is carried.

Generally speaking, whenever a bag cargo is carried, all bare iron work is covered with matting or burlap in addition to the permanent and temporary dunnage already mentioned. All dunnage wood should be kept clean and dry.

Cargo Derricks

Although some ships are fitted with cranes for handling their cargoes, derricks, or 'cargo booms' as they are sometimes called, are still the most favoured.

The derrick itself is made of tested tubular steel

12–15 inches in diameter and varying in length from about 20–25 feet.

There are several methods of rigging derricks, and to illustrate one of these we have chosen the 'Span and Chain Preventer' rig (see Fig. 57). It will be noticed that the derrick is free to move in any direction due to the heel being stepped into a 'gooseneck' arrangement; also that when the derrick is in the required position it is kept rigid by means of two guys.

Topping or Lowering Derricks
To do this safely and efficiently six men are required to be stationed as follows:

One man on each guy, one on the preventer guy, one driving the winch, one attending to the topping lift wire, and one man to unshackle and re-shackle the chain preventer. When all is ready the preventer guy is let go and as much of the cargo runner as possible is taken off the winch. The topping lift wire is passed through the lead block and a few turns are taken around the drum of the winch. The men on the guys stand by to slacken or tighten them as required and a gentle heave is taken on the topping lift wire. As soon as the weight of the derrick is taken on the topping lift wire, the chain preventer is unshackled and the derrick hoisted or lowered into the required position by the topping lift wire. When the derrick is in place, the chain preventer is shackled on again and the topping lift wire eased off until the preventer is taking the weight of the derrick. The preventer guys are then set up tightly.

The 'Union Purchase'
On most ships at least two derricks are fitted at each hatchway, and a very popular method of working

cargo is to have one derrick guyed to plumb the centre of the hatch and the other reaching out over the ship's side. The cargo runners of both derricks are shackled together, and to a short length of chain and a cargo hook. This method of working is known as the 'Union Purchase' or 'Married Gear'.

The Double Lift

This is another method of handling cargo where, in the case of loading, one derrick lifts off the quay on to the deck, and the inboard derrick picks up from the deck and lowers into the hold.

The disadvantage of this method is that the derrick which is plumbed overside needs to be a swinging derrick and this is not always convenient.

The Single Derrick

A single derrick is only used for handling cargo on very small ships. On a larger ship the process of continually heaving the derrick inboard and outboard would put a terrific strain on the gear which would not be compensated for even if there were winches available to rig steam guys.

Jumbo Derricks

More often than not, a ship is equipped with one or two special derricks called 'Jumbos' which are used for handling very heavy cargoes. The safe working load of ordinary derricks is usually 5 tons, but jumbo derricks have a safe working load of between 20 and 50 tons. Very occasionally, a ship is fitted with heavy lift derricks which have a safe working load exceeding 100 tons. Jumbo derricks when not in use stand upright and are lashed to the mast with a canvas covering over their top blocks. Ordinary derricks are lowered down and rest in crutches fitted at the side of the hatches.

Preventer Guys
When working cargo a great strain comes on the outboard guys, so to ease this strain, and as a safety

SINGLE CARGO DERRICK

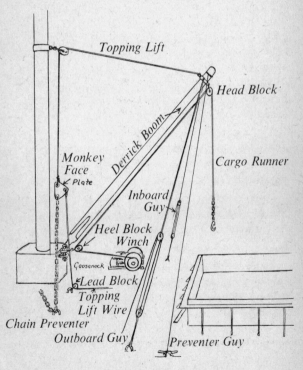

Fig 57

measure in case the rope tackle of the guy should part, a preventer or 'lazy' guy is used (see Fig. 57).

Bipod Masts

Since the days of sail, masts have only been required to carry signal yards, wireless aerials, navigation lights, etc., and are a means of support for the topping lifts of cargo derricks. In order to take the stresses placed on the masts during the pitching and rolling motion of the ship and the strains when working derricks, they were ably supported by 'standing rigging' consisting of shrouds and stays. This standing rigging invariably interfered with the efficient working distances of the derricks, and over the years the number of shrouds have been reduced by using shorter and stronger lower masts with telescopic topmasts. The present-day trend for most newly constructed ships is to use shroudless 'bipod' mast structures, which are strongly made of steel, usually welded to the main deck and capable of supporting very heavy lifts. They serve the four ordinary derricks, and a heavy-lift derrick is situated centrally between the two parts of the mast structure for serving the hatches on both sides. Control positions are built in with the mast structure, one on each part, giving a clear vision when working cargo.

Deck Cranes

Another popular method which is replacing the derrick is the use of purpose built cranes, hydraulically or electrically operated, which may either be used in a fixed position over a hatch or travel along rails to work at both ends of a hatch.

Cargo Gear

Cargo is handled by a variety of different pieces of equipment, of which the following are the most commonly seen and used.

Cargo Slings or Strops
These are made of pieces of 3- to 4-inch rope about 6 fathoms long, the ends of which are joined in a short splice. Slings or strops are used for all general cargo.

Cement Slings (see Fig. 58)
These are the same as ordinary slings with a piece of canvas about 4 feet by $1\frac{1}{2}$ feet sewn into the middle as illustrated. These slings can also be used for bag cargoes other than cement.

A CEMENT SLING

Canvas

Fig 58

Car Slings
These are made of about 2-inch wire. Two are needed, one each for the back and front wheels of the vehicle. Before the car is hoisted, large straw-filled cushions are inserted by the sides of each mudguard.

Chain Slings
A length of chain with a hook at one end and a large link at the other. They are used for handling heavy, coarse goods such as iron bars and girders, sheet iron

or machinery, etc. The sling is passed twice around the material and the end hooked on to the chain. The big link is then hooked on to the cargo runner and the chain tightens around the load as it is lifted.

Snotters
A length of rope or wire with an eye spliced in each end. The rope or wire is passed around the package and one eye rove through the other.

Can Hooks (see Fig. 59)
Used for lifting drums, casks, barrels, etc. The hooks fit under the chime of the cask at each end, the weight of the cask keeping the hooks in place. Several of these can be used at once for lifting small drums.

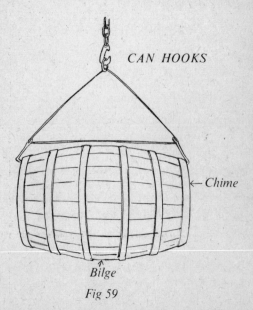

CAN HOOKS

← *Chime*

↑
Bilge

Fig 59

Nets

These can be of rope or small gauge wire and are useful for picking up small irregular-shaped packages. These are invariably used when a ship is taking stores aboard for a voyage.

Trays

A strong wooden tray is used for handling small regular-shaped packages. It is slung by a four-legged bridle made of rope or wire.

Tubs

Steel tubs with a capacity of about 1 ton are sometimes used where mechanical 'grabs' are not available for the handling of cargoes such as phosphates, iron ore, coal, etc.

Baskets

Rattan cane baskets with a capacity of about 5 cwt are often used after discharging a cargo for removing rubbish and cargo 'sweepings' from the holds.

Distribution and Stowage of Cargo

If possible, the weights of cargo should be evenly distributed. Too much bottom weight will cause the vessel to be 'stiff' in a seaway, which means she will roll quickly and perhaps violently from side to side causing much strain on the vessel. On the other hand, if the weights are brought too high, this will tend to make the vessel top heavy or 'tender' and in a seaway she will flop sluggishly from side to side, possibly with the danger of capsizing.

All cargo must be securely stowed, and lashed

where necessary, to prevent danger of it shifting at sea should the vessel encounter bad weather.

Care must be taken to see that there is no pilfering or damage whilst the cargo is being loaded and stowed.

Foodstuffs must never be stowed in contact with, or in close proximity to, goods which may taint them with their fumes. For instance, cases of tea would be easily tainted if stowed too close to soap, petrol or palm kernels, etc.

Cargo for different destinations should be clearly marked and if possible stowed in different compartments.

Liquids should never be stowed over solids.

Dangerous chemicals, oils and acids, etc., should be stowed on the open deck so that they can be quickly jettisoned, i.e. thrown overboard, if necessary. They should be well lashed down and protected from the rays of the sun with a light coloured tarpaulin.

Inflammable goods should be stowed well clear of engine room bulkheads.

Bales of cotton or wool should be treated with respect as they are highly inflammable. When loading these commodities there must be no smoking and fire hoses must be rigged ready at the hatchways.

Plate glass, slabs of marble, sheets of asbestos, etc., should be stowed on their ends resting athwartships. Rolls of paper and newsprint should be stowed on end.

Barrels, casks, etc., must be stowed with the bung uppermost and the bilge (see Fig. 59) of the barrel clear of the deck. This is achieved by driving wedges called 'quoins' under each quarter of the barrel.

Ventilation of Cargo

Cowl Ventilators

Fig. 60 illustrates the most common type of cargo ventilator, and shows also the passage of the air into the tween decks and the lower hold. There are at least two of these ventilators to each cargo compartment, and where the cargo is gaseous and gives off a gas lighter than air these ventilators may both be kept turned with their backs to the wind. When it is required to ventilate through the cargo, the lee ventilator (the one furthest from the wind) is turned to face the wind and the weather ventilator is placed back to wind. This ensures a good circulation in the lower hold and the tween deck.

In the case of heavy rain or when the vessel is shipping spray or water, all ventilators should be turned with their backs to the wind. In very heavy weather the vessel may ship water over the bows and in this case it may be necessary to unship the ventilators at No. 1 hatch, and also to plug and cover these ventilator coamings.

Surface Ventilation

Nearly all general cargoes are ventilated in the manner just described and this is known as through ventilation.

With some cargoes this type of ventilation can be dangerous, and a very good example of this is coal. On no account must air be passed through a cargo of coal. Heating would occur due to the coal absorbing oxygen from the air and there would be danger of spontaneous combustion.

All ventilators are turned back to wind and canvas

covers are placed over the cowls. Every day when the weather is reasonably fine, the hatchboards at the side of the hatches are lifted and air allowed to pass over the surface of the coal to remove the gases. This is known as surface ventilation.

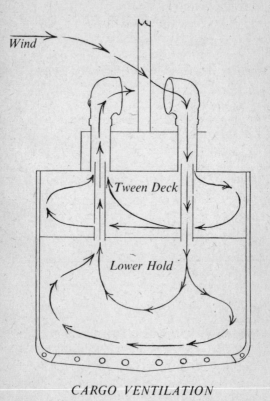

CARGO VENTILATION

Fig 60

Ventilation of Tankers

Narrow tube ventilators, which are sometimes taken to a considerable height, are used to admit air or allow gas to escape. These ventilators may be opened or closed and are fitted with regulators which help to prevent loss by evaporation of spirit cargoes. When the tanks have been freshly emptied, the gases remaining are expelled by steam injectors or drawn off by suction fans.

Draught Marks and Load Lines

Draught and Draught Marks

Draught means the distance in feet from the waterline to the lowest part of the keel.

On either side of the bow and stern of a ship, numbers are cut in and painted. These numbers are 6 inches high and are spaced 6 inches apart, enabling one at any given moment to ascertain the draught. These numbers are called draught marks. When the water line is at the bottom of a number this indicates an even foot of draught, for example:

The bottom of the 16 feet mark indicates	16′ 0″
Half way up the 16 feet mark indicates	16′ 3″
The top of the 16 feet mark indicates	16′ 6″
Half way between the top of the 16 and the bottom of the 17 indicates	16′ 9″

When the waterline is anywhere between these above mentioned marks, it can usually be judged to the nearest half inch, and in this respect it is worth remembering that the numbers are exactly 1 inch thick.

If the ship is listed either way, then the draught must be read on both sides and the mean taken.

Load Lines

Nowadays no ship is allowed to sail if she is overloaded, and to prevent overloading all ships are marked amidships with a 'plimsoll line' and 'load lines' (see Fig. 61). Immediately above the plimsoll line and level with the main deck is a line called the 'deck line'. The distance between the water line and

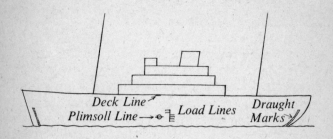

Fig 61

the deck line is called the 'freeboard'. The freeboard at maximum load draught is the distance from the plimsoll line to the deck line. The amount of freeboard a ship shall have is decided by an assigning authority and the initial letters of that authority will be found alongside the disc of the plimsoll line.

The assigning authorities are Lloyd's Register (L.R.), British Corporation (B.C.) and the Board of Trade (B.O.T.). The letters alongside the load line in Fig. 62 can be interpreted as follows:

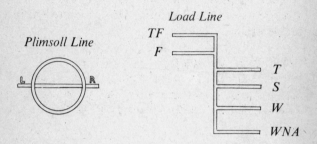

PLIMSOLL LINE and LOAD LINES

Fig 62

T F	Tropical Fresh Water
F	Fresh Water
T	Tropical Salt Water
S	Summer
W	Winter
W N A	Winter North Atlantic

This means, for example, that a ship trading in the North Atlantic in wintertime would only be able to load until the waterline reached the top edge of the W N A line, and a ship loading in tropical fresh water would be able to submerge to the top edge of the T F line.

All these lines are 1 inch thick.

Tonnages

People often refer to a ship as being so many tons
without really understanding the meaning of tonnage
as applied to ships. Usually they are referring to the
'gross tonnage' of the ship, but there are several other
methods of ship measurement which are worth con-
sideration.

Under Deck Tonnage

This is the total internal volume of the ship from the
top of the ceiling or double bottom to the underside
of the main deck reckoned at 100 cubic feet to the
ton.

Gross Tonnage

This is the under deck tonnage plus the tonnage of all
the enclosed spaces above the main deck, which is
reckoned at 100 cubic feet to the ton.

Net Tonnage

This is the tonnage remaining after various deduc-
tions have been made in respect of the engine room,
ballast tanks and crew spaces, etc., from the gross
tonnage.

Deadweight Tonnage

This is the total number of tons (2240 lb) of cargo
and stores, etc., that the vessel is capable of carrying
when loaded to the top of her summer mark.

Displacement Tonnage

This is the actual weight of the ship and contents, or
the number of tons of water displaced by the vessel
when floating at her load draught.

CHAPTER 10

SPEED AND SOUNDINGS

Speed and Distance

A ship's speed through the water can be ascertained roughly by counting the number of revolutions of the propeller per minute. The number of revolutions which are equal to 1 knot of speed will vary from ship to ship, depending in the main upon the size and 'pitch' of the propeller. Pitch means the distance the propeller will move the ship through the water with one revolution.

When a ship is on a long voyage the speed is not so important as knowing the actual distance the ship moves towards her destination from day to day. The exact distance is calculated from sextant observations of heavenly bodies, but greatly assisting in these calculations is an instrument called a Patent Log which gives the navigator a reasonably close approximation of the distance run.

The Patent Log

Most vehicles are fitted with an instrument which records on their dashboards the total number of miles they have travelled. The patent log is an instrument which serves the same purpose for a ship by recording the number of nautical miles travelled through the water.

The registering machinery is contained in a

cylindrical brass case fitted with a dial graduated from 0-100 miles. There are also two smaller dials, one showing tenths and the other hundreds of miles (see Fig. 63).

The brass case is clamped either to a rail at the stern of the ship or to a long boom which extends out amidships, and to the end of the case is attached a special plaited line called a log line which is towed through the water. Submerged at the end of this line is a brass rotator which keeps the line revolving and the mechanism working at a speed which varies directly with the speed of the ship. Close to the registering machinery a large flywheel, known as a Governor, is introduced into the line. This keeps the line and mechanism revolving at a uniform speed (see Fig. 64).

Streaming the Log. This is the term used for putting the log out. First of all the brass case, or 'log clock' as it is called, is clamped into its fitting and the governor is hooked on. The rotator is attached to one end of the line, and the line is flaked up and down the deck to ensure that it will run out freely. The other end of the line is hooked on to the governor, and the rotator is thrown over the side well clear of any obstructions and the line paid out.

Hauling in a Log from the Stern. Pull in some slack and unhook the line from the governor. As the line is hauled in on one side of the ship, pay it out again on the other side to free it of kinks. Finally, haul the line in again and coil it down left-handed.

Hauling in a Log from a Midship Boom. A small grapnel is thrown out over the line near the rotator

DIAL OF PATENT LOG

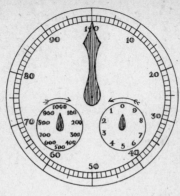

Fig 63

THE PATENT LOG EQUIPMENT

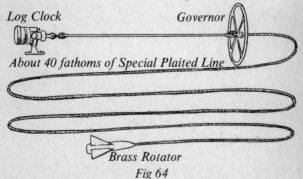

Log Clock   Governor

About 40 fathoms of Special Plaited Line

Brass Rotator

Fig 64

and the line brought up on board. Care must be exercised to see that the rotator is not damaged when being hauled up the side of the ship.

Setting the Log. On most ships the log is set back to zero at noon every day. This is done because the ship's position is plotted each day at this time and it is convenient to have the log reset so that the ship's progress can be followed more easily from watch to watch. The large pointer should always be moved in a clockwise direction. The smaller dials are rarely used or even referred to.

Electric Logs

Some patent logs are fitted with an electrical attachment which makes it possible for a repeater log to be placed in the chart room convenient for the navigator.

The 'Chernikeef' Log

This consists of a tube which extends out from the bottom of the ship and houses an impeller. The forward motion of the ship causes the water to turn the blades of the impeller at a speed which is in proportion to the speed of the ship. It is a very sensitive instrument which can be adapted to record both distance and actual speed at any given moment.

Soundings

When a vessel is approaching or near the coast it is essential that she should know the depth of water beneath the keel. There are four methods of sounding all of which are known as 'taking soundings'.

The Hand Lead and Line

This is used for taking soundings in shallow water. It consists of a four-stranded unkinkable line just over 20 fathoms long, with a lead attached to one end weighing about 7 or 8 lb. The line is marked as follows:

At	2 fathoms	2 strips of leather.
,,	3 ,,	3 ,, ,,
,,	5 ,,	A piece of white linen.
,,	7 ,,	,, ,, ,, red bunting.
,,	10 ,,	,, ,, ,, leather with a hole in it.
,,	13 ,,	,, ,, ,, blue serge.
,,	15 ,,	,, ,, ,, white linen.
,,	17 ,,	,, ,, ,, red bunting
,,	20 ,,	,, ,, ,, cord with two knots in it.

Linen, bunting and serge are used so that a leadsman can tell the soundings at night by touch.

The fathoms which are not marked, i.e. 1, 4, 6, 8, 9, 11, 12, 14, 16, 18 and 19, are known as 'deeps'.

Taking a Cast with the Hand Lead. On each side of the ship are small portable platforms called 'chains'. The lead is hove from the side where the shallowest water is expected, and the leadsman when entering the chains should make sure that the stanchions and lines surrounding the platform are secure. The end of the leadline is made fast and then, leaning well out over the platform, the line is grasped at about the 2 fathom mark.

Facing the direction in which the ship is travelling, the lead is swung pendulum fashion until sufficient momentum is gained to heave the lead forward into the water. As soon as the lead touches the bottom, the strain will come off the line, and when the line is up and down beneath the platform the sounding is called out to the bridge.

Note: Normally, when soundings are being taken with the hand lead, the vessel is proceeding slowly and navigating with caution by reason of her being in shallow water. However, if she is not proceeding slowly, added momentum can be given to the lead by swinging it two or three full turns over the head.

Calling the Soundings. At each cast of the lead the leadsman calls out the sounding to the bridge, always naming the nearest number of fathoms last as follows:

Sounding		Call
5	fathoms	By the mark 5.
$5\frac{1}{4}$	,,	And a quarter 5.
$5\frac{1}{2}$	,,	And a half 5.
$5\frac{3}{4}$	,,	A quarter less 6.
6	,,	By the deep 6.
$6\frac{1}{4}$	,,	And a quarter 6.
$6\frac{1}{2}$	,,	And a half 6.
$6\frac{3}{4}$	,,	A quarter less 7.
7	,,	By the mark 7, etc.

The Deep Sea Lead

The deep sea leadline is 100 fathoms long and is attached to a lead which weighs between 28 and 30 lb. It is marked in exactly the same manner as the hand lead up to 20 fathoms, and thereafter every tenth fathom is marked by an additional knot and the

5-fathom marks in between are identified by a single knot. Thus at each of 25, 35, 45, 55, etc., there is a piece of cord with one knot in it, and at 30 fathoms a piece of cord with 3 knots, at 40 fathoms 4 knots, and so on.

Sounding with the Deep Sea Lead. This is very rarely used nowadays, but should the occasion arise then a good plan is to station a man in the chains as before, and have a second man to run the lead and line outside of everything up to the bows. When all is ready the ship should be almost stopped. The man in the bow would warn the man in the chains by shouting out 'watch there watch' and then drop the lead over the side. A small block would be needed to heave the lead back aboard.

Mechanical Sounding Machines

The two methods of sounding just described are only used in the event of a breakdown in the more modern sounding machines. There are two types of sounding machines and most deep sea ships are equipped with both.

The Patent Sounding Machine

On modern ships the sounding machine is fitted on the boat deck amidships. It consists of a small hand winch, the drum of which holds about 300 fathoms of fine wire. The end of the wire is attached to a lead sinker and, to keep the lead and wire away from the ship's side, it is passed out over a pulley at the end of a boom similar to a log boom. Just behind the sinker a brass case containing a long glass tube is attached to the wire. The glass tube is open at one end and the inside is coated with chromate of silver which the sea water reacts upon, changing it to chloride of silver. The pressure of water increases proportionately with the depth; therefore, the amount of water forced into the tube will indicate the depth to which it has been submerged. This depth is ascertained accurately by comparing the tube with a boxwood scale provided for the purpose.

There are several variations in the method of manufacture of patent sounding machines, but they are all practically the same in principle.

The Echo Sounding Machine

This is the method most favoured for obtaining soundings. The Echo Sounding Machine is operated simply by turning a switch, the result obtained being very accurate.

It is based on the principle that sound travels through water at a fixed uniform speed. The echo sounding equipment transmits a sound wave which is reflected back from the seabed and received by a sensitive instrument known as a hydrophone.

The time taken for the sound wave to be transmitted and received is divided by two and translated into distance by an ingenious electrical mechanism. The sounding in feet or fathoms can then be seen at a glance on the dial of the recording machine situated in the chartroom. Instead of a dial recording, some machines provide a permanent record by being fitted with a roll of special paper and a stylus pen.

These machines have been so perfected and are so sensitive that trawlers often use them for finding the depth of shoals of fish.

CHAPTER 11

SHIPS' LIFEBOATS

The size of lifeboats varies generally between 24 and 40 feet in length, according to the type and tonnage of the vessel carrying them. They must be fitted with buoyancy tanks made of yellow metal and filled with kapok, and there must be at least one cubic foot of buoyancy tank per person which the boat is certified to carry. A lifeboat must have a capacity of not less than 125 cubic feet, and the weight of any lifeboat when fully laden with equipment and persons (allowing 165 lb per person) must not exceed 20 tons. All ships' lifeboats are double-ended.

Average Weights and Sizes

On the average foreign-going merchantman, a lifeboat is about 30 feet long, carries about 30 persons and weighs about 5 tons when fully laden. A lifeboat's dimensions and her cubic capacity are cut into the stem.

Ascertaining the Number of People a Lifeboat will Carry

If the cubic capacity of a boat is not known it can be ascertained with reasonable accuracy by the simple formula:

Length × Breadth × Depth × ·6=Cubic Capacity.

Each person in a boat is allowed 10 cubic feet of space; therefore, the cubic capacity divided by 10 gives the number of persons a boat can carry. Do not forget that one of the cubic feet allowed per person is taken away for buoyancy tank space, as mentioned in the first paragraph of this Chapter.

The ·6 is known as the coefficient of fineness and represents the ratio the shape of the boat bears to a rectangular block of the same dimensions. Thus in the case of, say, a fine-lined yacht the coefficient of fineness would be ·5 or even less.

Number of Lifeboats Carried

On a passenger ship there must be sufficient boats to accommodate the total number of persons she is certified to carry. On an ordinary foreign-going cargo ship or tanker, etc., there must be the same number of boats on either side of the ship, each side being sufficient in itself to accommodate the total number of the crew.

Identification of Lifeboats

Each lifeboat carried by a ship is given a distinguishing number, the boats on the starboard side being odd numbered and on the port, even numbered. The numbering always starts from forward; thus the boat furthest forward on the starboard side would be number 1 boat and the boat furthest forward on the port side would obviously be number 2 boat. On some larger passenger ships, lifeboats are stowed in pairs one over the other. These are numbered in the same manner but are designated 'a' and 'b'.

Single and Double Banking

When only one oar is pulled from each seat (thwart) on alternate sides of the boat this is known as 'single banking'. When an oar is pulled from each side of each thwart this is said to be 'double banking'.

Types of Boats

There are three types of wooden boats which are named according to the manner in which their planking is arranged:

1. *The Clinker or Clencher Built Boat*

In boats of this type the planks run fore and aft and overlap each other, giving an uneven surface on both the inside and outside of the boat. Almost all ships' lifeboats are of this type.

2. *The Carvel Built Boat*

The planks of a carvel built boat also run fore and aft, but in this case the planks are not over-lapped but fitted close up against each other, giving a smooth flush finish both inside and out. This type of construction is usually found on light racing craft.

3. *The Diagonal Built Boat*

This type of boat has double planking, with the planks of the outer skin running diagonally across the planks of the inner skin, a flush finish being achieved both inside and out. The double skin of the boat makes for greater strength, and this type of construction is found on larger boats, particularly on larger racing craft.

Steel Lifeboats

These boats are built up of riveted or welded steel plates. On tankers it is compulsory to carry steel boats because of the danger of fire. Approved steel boats may be carried by any ship instead of the more conventional wooden ones. This type of boat is particularly popular in the American merchant fleet.

Motor Lifeboats

All foreign-going merchantmen carry at least one motor lifeboat, the purpose of this boat being to tow the non-power boats safely away from a sinking or foundering vessel. A motor boat is also provided with portable radio equipment which is kept in a convenient position ready to be placed in the boat in an emergency.

Jolly Boats

In addition to her lifeboats a ship often carries a small, double-ended boat called a jolly boat. This boat is used in port for taking people backwards and forwards from the shore should the vessel be at anchor. It is also often used when painting the ship's hull. A jolly boat is frequently stowed at the stern of the ship.

Construction of a Clinker Built Lifeboat

The following should be studied in conjunction with Figs. 65 and 66.

The backbone of the boat is formed by a single straight piece of timber called the *Keel*. The ends of the keel are joined to the *Stem* and the *Sternpost*, and each of these three components is visible on the outside of the completed boat. On top of the keel is the *Hogpiece*, and it will be noticed in Fig. 65 that this is shaped to take the lowest plank known as the *Garboard Strake*. On top of the hogpiece and running transversely are the *Timbers* or ribs. The planks of the boat are fitted to the outside of these timbers which are spaced about 5 inches apart. Keeping

TRANSVERSE SECTION OF
A CLINKER BUILT LIFEBOAT

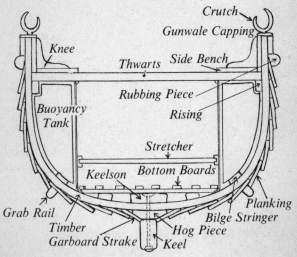

Fig 65

the timbers in place on the bottom of the boat is the *Keelson* which runs longitudinally in the same manner as the keel and hogpiece. The ends of the keelson are joined to boomerang-shaped pieces of wood called *Deadwoods*, and the ends of the deadwoods are continued upwards and connected to the stem and sternpost by pieces of timber called *Aprons*. The planks of the boat terminate where the aprons and deadwoods are joined to the stem and sternpost. At the bilge (or turn of the boat) a piece of timber running longitudinally is fitted for extra strength, this being known as a *Bilge Stringer*. Running right around the inside of the boat a few inches below the *Gunwale,* i.e. the top edge of the planking, is a continuous seat known as the *Side Bench*. This side bench is supported at intervals of 2 or 3 feet by wooden or metal angle pieces called *Knees*. Underneath the side benches spaced about 3 feet apart

LONGITUDINAL SECTION OF A LIFEBOAT

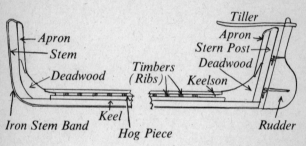

Fig 66

and running transversely are the *Thwarts* or rowing seats. These thwarts are supported underneath at each side of the boat by timbers very similar to bilge stringers which are known as *Risings*. The yellow metal buoyancy tanks are fitted underneath the side benches on each side of the boat. Just below the gunwale on the outside of the boat there is a rounded wooden beading running the whole length on both sides; this is known as the *Rubbing Piece*. This, as the name implies, is to protect the sides of the boat when she is alongside a ship or quay, etc. Fitted to the underside of the rubbing piece is a looped rope which acts as a *Grab Line* for supporting people in the water.

Most boats tend to let in a little water between the seams of the planking, especially in the case of a lifeboat which may have been out of the water for a long time, and so for the comfort of the people in the boat the bottom is covered with portable wooden frames known as *Bottom Boards*. On top of these bottom boards and extending from side to side in front of each thwart are pieces of timber called *Stretchers*. These are provided for the oarsmen to brace their feet against when rowing.

An interesting feature about the construction of clinker built boats is that the planking is secured first, and the timbers or ribs (made of elm, ash or oak) are steamed into shape and placed in afterwards.

Copper nails only are used for fastening plank edges, etc. Screws and bolts are usually galvanised, but on better-class boats these are solid brass. The use of these materials is necessary because of the effect of sea water on bare iron or steel.

Preservation of Boats

Should the case arise where a vessel has to be abandoned on the high seas, her boats become the only means of saving life; and for this reason alone they should be maintained at all times in a first-rate condition of repair and seaworthiness.

The useful life of a boat is almost directly proportional to the amount it is used. The more a boat is put into the water and used, the longer will be its seaworthy life, and every opportunity should be taken to do this. If this is not possible, then the next best thing is occasionally to half fill the boat with water, especially in very hot or dry climates. If the boat is not placed in water or half filled occasionally, the planks will contract, thus opening the seams.

Caulking Boats

If a boat is treated in the above manner and still continues to leak badly, it is possible that she may require 'caulking'. This simply means filling in the seams of the boat with a water resistant material. The cheapest caulking material is the 'teased' and tarred fibres of rope known as oakum. The best thing to use, though, is caulking cotton, which can be obtained in 1-lb balls from any merchant dealing in ship's stores.

A clinker built boat must only be caulked in the garboard strake next to the keel. If caulking is attempted between the ordinary seams, it will result in forcing the planks apart and the boat will leak worse than before. For these seams it is recommended that a mixture of lead paint and putty be used.

Painting Boats

Always use the best paint available; one good coat of paint is better than two or three inferior coats. Next to the bare wood of the boat a paint with a heavy lead content should be used. Two and sometimes three coats of this may be needed before the final topcoat is applied. A good hard gloss paint is unbeatable as a topcoat; it is decorative and stands up well to sea-water and hard wear.

If possible, choose a fine sunny day for painting. Apply the paint sparingly, but avoid 'holidays', i.e.

bare patches in the paintwork. Make sure that with each coat all joins and seams are well covered. When one coat has dried and the next coat to be applied is of the same colour, it is a good idea to tint it to prevent 'holidays'.

Lifeboat Equipment

The following equipment is standard and compulsory in all ship's lifeboats. For the purpose of easy reference this has been divided into four sections, as follows:

1. *Sailing Gear*

Oars. A full single-banked complement of oars and two spare oars, also a steering oar which can be used for steering in the event of the rudder being lost or damaged. This oar is at least 1 foot longer than the other oars and has the blade painted white. All oars are laid in the boat with the blades forward, except the steering oar which is laid with the blade aft.

Crutches. Galvanised U-shaped pieces of metal which support the oars in the rowing position on the gunwale. There is a set and a half of these attached to the boat by lanyards, i.e. light lines.

Rudder and Tiller. Fitted to the stern of the boat by means of 'pintles' and 'gudgeons' (see Fig. 67).

Mast. The mast must be a Norway spar not exceeding two-thirds the length of the boat.

Sails. One sail if under 25 feet in length, and two sails if the boat exceeds this length. These sails are coloured bright red, and marked with an identification letter and number in white.

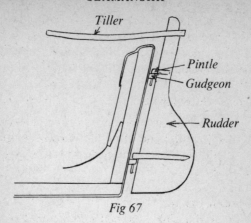

Fig 67

Plugs. Two plugs for each plug hole fitted with lanyards or chains.

Painters. A painter is a rope about 3 inches in circumference and not less than 20 fathoms long. Two of these are provided for a lifeboat—one at each end. The function of painters is to steady the boat after launching until all persons are aboard. The painters are given a long lead from the bow and stern of the lifeboat to the gunwale of the ship.

Boathooks. A long pole with a hook at one end. At least one must be provided, but two are carried in the case of motor boats. They are used to 'fend' the boat away from the ship's side during lowering and to give the boat the final sheer away from the ship when all is ready. Also to hold the boat alongside a quay, jetty, buoy, etc.

Compass. A liquid compass fitted in a binnacle with means of illumination.

Charts, etc. A complete set of ocean charts carried in a waterproof wallet, together with navigational tables, protractor, writing paper, pencil and eraser.

Sea Anchor (see Fig. 68). This is simply a tapered canvas bag fitted with a riding line and a tripping line. In rough weather the boat drifts astern of it, and it helps to keep the boat's head to wind and sea. Attached to the sea anchor is a small oil bag which is filled with heavy oil. This bag has been pricked with a sail needle and this allows some of the oil to drift back to the boat. The effect of oil on water is to modify the breaking of waves.

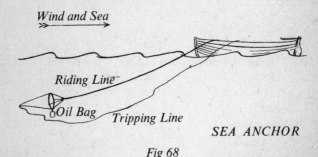

Wind and Sea

Riding Line

Oil Bag   Tripping Line

SEA ANCHOR

Fig 68

2. *Signals*
Oil Lamp. An approved type of lantern with sufficient oil to burn for eight hours.

Matches. Special slow burning matches contained in a watertight case.

Electric Torch. This must be of a type suitable for signalling, and is supplied with two spare batteries and bulbs.

Signalling Mirror. Used for daytime signalling in sunlight.

Red Flares. Twelve 'five star red flares' carried in a watertight container and used to attract attention at night time.

Smoke Floats. Two buoyant canisters giving off orange-coloured smoke when ignited. Used as a daytime signal to attract attention.

Radio Equipment. This is carried for use on motor boats and, as mentioned before, is only placed in the boat in an emergency.

3. Rations

The following are the minimum amounts required to be provided per person the boat is certified to carry:

Water	112 oz ($\frac{3}{4}$ gallon)	
Biscuits	14	,,
Barley Sugar ...	14	,,
Condensed Milk ...	14	,,

Food Tanks. Watertight metal food tanks are fitted underneath the thwarts.

Water Containers. Generally made of metal and also fitted under the thwarts. The water in these containers needs to be frequently changed to ensure that it is always clean and fresh.

Dipper. This is a small cylindrical enamelled container which is attached to a lanyard or chain and is used for dipping the water out of the containers.

Drinking Vessels. Three rustproof drinking vessels are provided, which are graduated in $\frac{1}{2}$, 1 and 2 ozs.

4. *Miscellaneous*

Baler. Made of galvanised iron and shaped like a very large soup ladle, this is used for bailing water out of the boat.

Pump. A semi-rotary pump is fitted to the side of the boat with an overside discharge and a movable intake beneath the bottom boards.

Oil Can. This contains one gallon of oil for use with the sea anchor.

Buckets. Two large galvanised iron buckets are provided.

Knife. One knife, fitted with a tin opener, is provided.

Hatchets. Two hatchets are provided, one at each end of the boat, attached by lanyards.

Heaving Lines. Two light heaving lines are carried.

Inventory. A list of all the equipment carried in the boat.

It may be worth mentioning that additional equipment in the form of blankets, brandy, fishing tackle, first-aid equipment, etc., is often provided by the ship's owners.

Boat Pulling

The handling of a boat under oars is an art which can only be acquired by actual practice. It can be a hard gruelling task or it can be pleasant exercise, according to the skill and experience of the crew.

A few hints here may be useful to the would-be oarsman. Firstly, get yourself into a comfortable position on the thwart and brace your legs against the stretcher. Grasp the oar with the hands a little apart and make sure that the oar is in a position in the crutch where it will have maximum leverage. Do not try to pull the oar towards you with your arms, but lean back at each stroke and let the weight of your body do the work. Keep your feet together on the stretcher, and your back and shoulders straight. Avoid crouching over the oar. Do not watch your oar but keep your eyes on the man in front of you, and follow each of his movements. All the crew of a boat sit facing aft except the 'coxswain' (the person in charge), who sits in the stern of the boat facing the crew. In a double-banked boat the two oarsmen nearest to the coxswain are known as the 'stroke oarsmen', and when rowing the other oarsmen take their timing from the port and starboard stroke respectively. Seamen candidates for the Board of Trade examination for 'Lifeboatmen's Certificates' take turns in the positions of coxswain, stroke and crewmen; and for these and others who wish to become proficient boatmen, the following orders given by the coxswain must be thoroughly understood.

Boat Orders

It will be assumed that the crew are ready and that the oars are lying in the boat with the blades forward.

'Toss Your Oars'

The oars are tossed up on end with the looms (see Fig. 69) resting on the bottom boards and the sharp ends of the blades facing fore and aft.

'Out Oars' or 'Down Oars'
The oars are lowered gently into the crutches, keeping
the shafts of them at right angles to the boat and the
blades parallel with the water.

'Rest on your Oars' or 'Oars'
Whenever this order is given the oars are brought
into the same position as for the order 'out oars'.

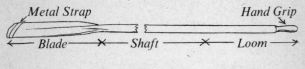

Fig 69

'Stand By'
At this order the crew lean aft and turn the blade of
the oar ready to take the first stroke.

'Give Way Together'
This is the order to start rowing. Timing is taken
from the stroke oars, with the port stroke taking time
from the starboard stroke.

'Way Enough'
This is the order to cease rowing, and if no further
order is given the crew will take one more stroke and
then toss oars. If the coxswain wishes the crew to
cease rowing without tossing oars, then the order
would be given as 'way enough, rest on your oars'.
The crew would then take one more stroke and come
to the rest position as described above.

'Hold Water'
This order is given if it is required to stop the boat

quickly. The blades of the oars are put vertically into the water and held firmly in that position.

'Hold Water Starboard' or 'Hold Water Port'

If when the boat is moving it is desired to turn quickly one way or the other, then the order 'hold water starboard' or 'hold water port' is given. Holding water on the starboard side will turn the boat quickly to starboard, and vice versa.

'Backwater'

This order may be given as 'backwater port', 'backwater starboard' or 'backwater together'. It simply means pushing the oars backwards through the water.

This order will only be given when the boat is moving slowly. If the boat was moving quickly, the effect of suddenly backwatering would probably break the blades of the oars. A boat will swing round very fast on the side which she is backwatered.

The order 'way enough' must always be given to a side or sides before backwatering.

'Bow'

This order is directed at the bow oarsman or the port bow oarsman in the case of a double banked boat. He tosses his oar, lays it in the boat and stands up with a boathook tossed, ready to go alongside.

'Boat Your Oars'

When the oars are in the tossed position and the coxswain wishes them to be laid in the boat, he gives the order 'boat your oars'. The oars are lowered gently down into the boat with the blades forward.

Note: The orders 'way enough', 'rest on your oars' and 'bow' are all executed one stroke after the order has been given. The coxswain should always give these orders when the oars are in the water.

Feathering Oars

Feathering an oar means to minimise the wind resistance when rowing. It is done by turning the wrists at the completion of each stroke and bringing the oar back over the water with the blade parallel to it.

Sculling a Boat

A small boat can be propelled and steered by a single oar at the stern. This requires a great deal of patient practice before the art is mastered. The blade of the oar is made to describe a figure-of-eight under the water by a side to side movement of the hands. What it actually does is to throw water astern in short jerky movements, thus propelling the boat ahead through the water. A square sterned boat is best suited to this purpose.

Sails

Boat sails are made of the best quality duck canvas and have rope sewn around the port edge to prevent fraying. This rope is always sewn to the port side of the sail to make the handling and hoisting of the sail, even on the darkest night, almost foolproof.

Parts of Sails

Each edge and corner of a sail is named (see Fig. 70) and these names should be committed to memory.

In the case of a lifeboat the head of the sail is laced to a wooden yard which is hoisted to the top of the mast by means of a 'traveller'. The traveller is simply a movable metal ring encircling the mast and attached to a halyard which leads through a block in the masthead. A hook is fitted to the traveller which enables the yard to be connected to it by means of a

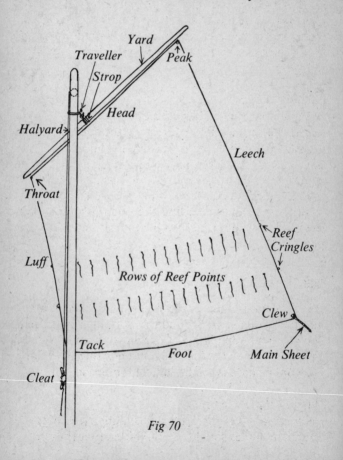

Fig 70

small strop. On each side of the sail there are one, two or three rows of small lines known as 'reef points', and sewn into the luff and leach of the sail at the same height as the reef points are small galvanised iron 'thimbles' called the 'reef cringles'. The purpose of reef points and cringles is to enable the sail to be shortened should it be so desired. Metal thimbles are also fitted at the peak, throat, tack and clew.

Two lines are attached to the clew of the jib-sail and one line to the clew of the lug-sail. These lines are termed the sheets.

Lifeboat Rigs

The shape and number of sails carried by a boat determines her type of rig. Small lifeboats are rigged with one large sail called a lugsail, and larger boats have a smaller sail in addition called a jib.

The Dipping Lug

When only one sail is carried, as on small lifeboats, this is usually a dipping lug (see Fig. 71).

With the wind aft, a dipping lug presents the whole area of the sail to the wind, and under these conditions it is very efficient. The disadvantage of the dipping lug is that, with each large alteration of course, the tack of the sail has to be let go and the yard dipped around the mast.

The Sloop Rigged Lifeboat or Standing Lug and Jib

This is the most common type of rig. Here the tack of the sail is made fast at the foot of the mast and there is no dipping to be done. This is obviously a great

DIPPING LUG

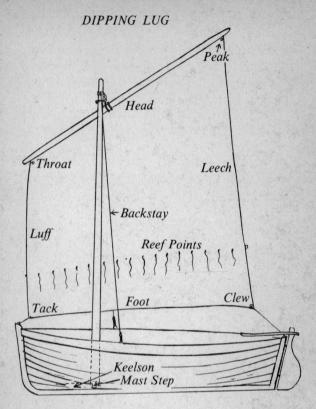

Fig 71

advantage where frequent alterations of course are necessary (see Fig. 72).

Rigging a Boat for Sailing

Stepping the Mast

The first thwart from forward in a boat is usually known as the *Sailing Thwart* and on the after end of

STANDING LUG AND JIB

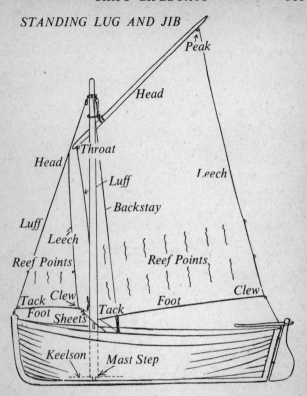

Fig 72

this is a clamp to hold the mast in position. Directly below this clamp a slot termed the *Mast Step* is cut into the keelson. The heel or base of the mast is shaped to fit into the mast step, and this is done before finally clamping the mast to the sailing thwart. When the mast is stepped in position a *Shroud* or

Backstay is set up on each side to hold the top of the mast firmly in place (see Figs. 71 and 72).

Hoisting the Sails

Lay the sail with the yard uppermost fore and aft down the middle of the boat making sure the roping will be on the port side when the sail is set.

Hook the tack to a ringbolt in the bow if a dipping lug, and take a couple of loose turns at the foot of the mast if a standing lug. The tack of a dipping lug is usually fitted with a spring clip or hook.

Place the strop around the yard and hook on to the traveller. This strop is placed one-third the length of the head of the sail from the throat in a dipping lug and one-quarter in a standing lug.

Stretch the sheet aft, order all hands to windward and hoist away.

The jib sail can be handled easily by one man. Make the tack fast in the bow, hook the jib halyard to the head of the sail, stretch the sheets aft and hoist away.

When all halyards are set up tightly, the tack of the lug sail should be tightened and made fast.

Sailing Terms

The art of managing and manoeuvring a boat under sail cannot be condensed into a few paragraphs. However, an understanding of the following boat sailing terms will give a solid groundwork to those interested in this rather complex art.

When a boat has the wind behind her with the sail trimmed full she is said to be *Running Free*. When altering course with the wind abaft the beam, the yard and sail swings from one side to the other and this is known as *Gybing*. When the wind is dead astern care must be taken to see that the boat does not *accidently gybe*, because in a stiff breeze the effect of the yard swinging violently from one side to

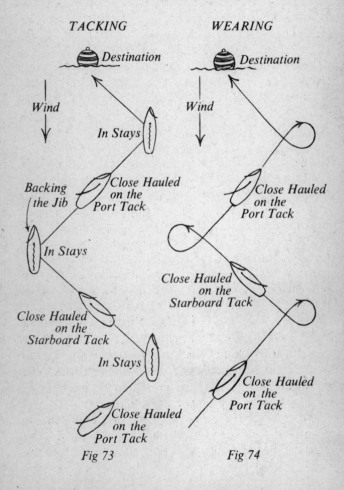

TACKING   *WEARING*

Destination   Destination

Wind   *Wind*

In Stays

Backing the Jib   *Close Hauled on the Port Tack*

Close Hauled on the Port Tack

In Stays   *Close Hauled on the Starboard Tack*

Close Hauled on the Starboard Tack

In Stays   *Close Hauled on the Port Tack*

Close Hauled on the Port Tack

Fig 73   Fig 74

the other could dismast or capsize the boat. A boat cannot sail directly into the wind, and in making for a destination which lies against the wind she adopts a zig-zag course which is known as *Tacking* (see Fig. 73). When a boat is tacking with the wind on the starboard side she is said to be on the *Starboard Tack,* and with the wind on the port side she is said to be on the *Port Tack*. Bearing in mind that a ship's lifeboat will probably be manned by a very inexperienced crew, the closest angle she can sail to the wind is about 70 degrees (roughly 6 points), and in this position she is said to be *Close Hauled*. According to which side the wind is on, a boat may be *Close Hauled on the Starboard Tack* or *Close Hauled on the Port Tack*. Just before altering from one tack to the other the order is usually given to *Up Helm* and this means that the tiller is pushed to windward, thus canting the rudder to leeward and the boat's head *Paying Off*. Paying off or *Filling* means that the boat is moving away from the wind and gathering speed as the sails fill. When the boat has sufficient speed the order to *Down Helm* is given. This means exactly the opposite to 'up helm'; the tiller is moved away from the wind and the boat's head moves to windward. When the boat is head to wind with the sails flapping she is said to be *In Stays,* and at this point the order is given to *Back the Jib,* i.e. pull out the jib sheet to one side to help her round on to the next tack. The coxswain often warns the crew that he is about to tack by giving the order *Ready About*.

Note: When the order 'up helm' or 'down helm' is given and the wind is dead astern, it is deemed to be that side of the tiller which the helmsman is steering from.

If a vessel comes up 'into stays' and will not 'pay off' on to the other tack, she is said to be *In Irons*. If she persistently refuses to *Go About,* she may be brought on to the other tack by *Wearing* (see Fig. 74). This should not be resorted to unless it is essential because, by wearing, the boat performs a loop-the-loop operation which loses a lot of ground, and in a strong breeze there is the added danger of an accidental gybe. An inexperienced crew attempting to 'wear' in a strong wind would be well advised to let the boat 'pay off' and then lower the sail right down until she is up on the other tack. *Luffing* or *Luffing Her Up* means putting the helm down when the boat is close hauled and bringing her up 'into stays'. This may be done to ease the speed of the boat without quite stopping her, or to ease the strain on the mast and rigging in a squall.

Reefing Sails

This means to shorten the sails, the purpose being that the stronger the wind, the less area of sail must be presented to it. To do this the boat must be stopped by bringing her head to wind. The tack and clew are then made fast to the appropriate reef cringles, the sail is bunched up (not rolled), the reef points tied and the sail re-set. Never leave reefing until the last moment; always try to anticipate future weather conditions and if possible be one move ahead of them.

If the wind becomes very strong take in the mainsail and run under the jib alone, and should the weather continue to get worse, the sea anchor should be used (see Fig. 68).

Sailing Hints

When a boat is under sail the proper place for the
crew is on the bottom boards abaft the mast. The
coxswain sits on the weather side, and any orders
given by him must be obeyed promptly and without
question.

Standing up or walking about in a boat should be
avoided; it upsets the trim of the boat and looks most
unseamanlike. The sheets must never be made fast,
but must be held in the hand ready to trim the sail at
a moment's notice. One reason for this is that the
wind is rarely constant from one quarter, but tends to
come in gusts which may vary in direction by as
much as 10 or 20 degrees. This variation means the
sail has to be constantly trimmed one way or the
other to ensure that the boat has maximum advantage of the wind.

Boat Hoisting and Lowering

When a boat is being hoisted or lowered, two arms
extend out from the ship over the water and to the top
of each of these arms the standing part of a three-
fold purchase is made fast. The movable blocks of the
purchase are made fast to hooks in the bow and stern
of the boat, and the hauling lines are led in the most
direct manner to the nearest winches.

The arms mentioned above are termed *Davits,* of
which there are three main types as follows:

1. *Radial or Swinging Davits*

These are the oldest and the simplest type, consisting
of two steel posts projecting upright from the boat-
deck and bending over at the top at right angles. With
the boat in the stowed position, the heads of these

davits point inboard. When the boat is required to be lowered, the boat and davits are swung outboard and extend over the water.

2. *Screw Davits*

This type of davit is very popular nowadays and is simple to operate. The arms of the davit are straight and are moved from the stowed position to the lowering position by turning a handle at each arm.

3. *Gravity Davits*

This type is the most complex, but perhaps the most speedy and efficient. A number of ships are fitted with them, particularly passenger ships. They depend for their action on gravity, the weight of the boat being made to do the work of swinging out and lowering. The boat rests in a cradle on an angled trackway, the cradle being the base of a davit arm which is almost semi-circular in shape. Each boat is controlled by a separate winch which is also fitted with a powerful handbrake.

Boat Drill

Every member of the crew of a ship is allotted a boat station and a particular job to do in the event of having to take to the boats. A list of these boat stations is posted in some conspicuous position and it is the duty of each seaman to familiarise himself with this, and with the type of boats and davits he will have to handle.

A boat drill is carried out weekly on most ships, at which lifejackets must be worn and the crew of each boat lined up and mustered. At these musters the boats are swung out into the lowering position to check that none of the working parts is seized up, and the crew are tested and questioned as to their knowledge of their particular station.

The key to all successful boatwork can be summarised as keenness, observance and strict obedience to orders.

Inflatable Liferafts

The Merchant Shipping Life-saving Appliances Rules of 1965 officially recognised the life-saving properties of inflatable liferafts and their installation aboard merchant ships has become universally accepted. The modern inflatable liferaft is recognised as being one of the most efficient—certainly the most rapid—means of evacuating personnel from a sinking vessel.

A TYPICAL 10-MAN LIFERAFT

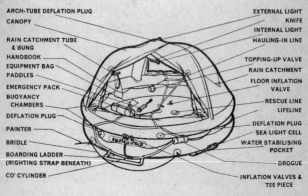

ARCH-TUBE DEFLATION PLUG
CANOPY
RAIN CATCHMENT TUBE & BUNG
HANDBOOK
EQUIPMENT BAG
PADDLES
EMERGENCY PACK
BUOYANCY CHAMBERS
DEFLATION PLUG
PAINTER
BRIDLE
BOARDING LADDER (RIGHTING STRAP BENEATH)
CO' CYLINDER

EXTERNAL LIGHT
KNIFE
INTERNAL LIGHT
HAULING-IN LINE
TOPPING-UP VALVE
RAIN CATCHMENT
FLOOR INFLATION VALVE
RESCUE LINE
LIFELINE
DEFLATION PLUG
SEA LIGHT CELL
WATER STABILISING POCKET
DROGUE
INFLATION VALVES & TEE PIECE

Fig. 75

All vessels under 500 tons can now dispense with lifeboats if properly fitted with inflatable liferafts meeting the requirements of the Board of Trade.

In addition to the required number of lifeboats, all passenger and cargo ships must now possess liferafts for at least 25% of the number of persons she is certified to carry.

The RFD Company of Godalming were pioneers in the development of liferafts and now produce marine liferafts ranging from 4- to 25-man capacities, all with a common vital characteristic—automatic self-inflation by means of a strong pull on the painter line.

Description

All RFD liferafts are constructed on the same basic principle—tubes of rubberised cotton fabric which are inflated with CO_2 gas. There are two super-imposed main buoyancy tubes, each separately inflated and each capable of supporting the full complement of passengers should one fail to inflate. In addition, the liferafts are provided with an automatically erected canopy which has an entrance at each end and is held in position by inflatable arches or centre support. The canopy has adjustable flaps at the entrances to control ventilation, and the floor of the raft can be manually inflated to provide insulation from the cold. Water pockets under the liferaft ensure stability and prevent the liferaft from being overturned in high winds and rough seas.

Other features of a liferaft are as follows:

Boarding ladders and hauling-in lines.
Water-activated cells to provide automatic internal light and external identification light.

Rescue line and quoit.
Paddles.
Floating safety knife.
Sea-anchor.
Equipment bag.
Emergency pack.

Equipment Bag
Each RFD liferaft is equipped with an equipment bag
containing:

Table of life-saving signals.
Torch with spare batteries.
Jug/cum baler.
Rubber plugs with cord.
Leak stoppers.
Spare drogue.
Repair kit.
Bellows pump.

Emergency Pack
The contents of the emergency pack which complies
with B.O.T. regulations includes:

First-aid kit.
Tins of water.
Anti-sea-sickness tablets.
Drinking cup/measure.
Parachute distress signals.
Fishing kit.
Hand flare signals.
Emergency rations.
Safety tin opener.
Whistle.
Heliograph (signalling mirror).
Sea survival pamphlet.

Liferaft Containers and Methods of Stowage

Liferafts are housed in various types of containers. One type consists of a waterproof hardwearing fabric valise, which is usually stowed either in collapsible

Valise and Deck Box Stowage

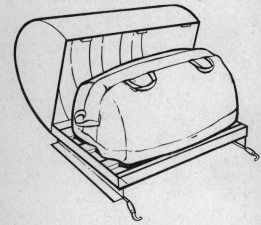

Fig 76

Deck Seat Stowage

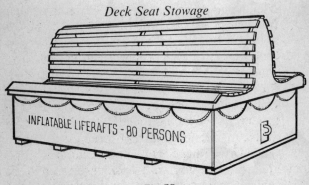

Fig. 77

deck boxes or in deck seats with an easily removable section to permit rapid access.

Another type is the glass fibre container stowed on a cradle bolted to the deck and secured by a 'V' strap and a Senhouse slip. It can also be fitted with a hydrostatic release which operates should the vessel sink before the release operation can be carried out.

Fibre Glass Container

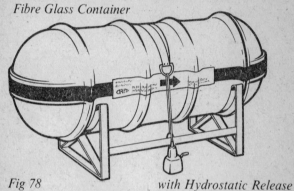

Fig 78   *with Hydrostatic Release*

Launching Liferafts

In an emergency every minute counts, and crews of ships should know where liferafts are situated and precisely what to do. The procedure for hand launching is as follows:

1. Remove cover and lashing securing valise or container.
2. Carry or roll it to the rail.
3. Pull out a length of operating cord and attach it to a strong point on the ship.
4. Throw the *whole container* overboard.
5. Pull on operating cord to start inflation.

Some vessels are fitted with a sloping ramp from which four or more containers can be released at the same time by operating a release mechanism.

Ramp Release

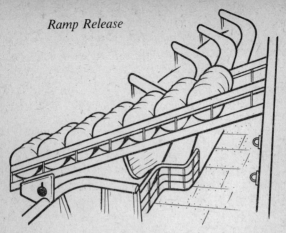

Fig 79

Boarding at Deck Level

Fig 80

A new system has been devised by the RFD Company specially for passenger ships with a high free-board in which the liferaft is inflated at deck level for easy boarding, lowered with its full complement from a special davit and automatically released from the davit line as it settles on the water.

Capsizing

In the unlikely event of a liferaft capsizing on launching, it is a comparatively easy matter for one man to right it. Grasp the strap at the position marked 'Right Here', clamber aboard the upturned raft and lean backwards. In this position it is possible to turn the raft the right way up.

Boarding

Boarding in an emergency must be as rapid as possible, and from the ship this is normally by means of boarding ladders, but personnel can jump onto the liferaft canopy avoiding others already aboard. Survivors in the water can board the raft by a webbing ladder or ramp, hauling themselves up head first. Disabled survivors should be grasped under the armpits and hauled aboard backwards.

When the liferaft is full, the painter should be cut and the raft moved to a safe distance with the paddles provided.

Once aboard, the following procedure should be carried out:

1. See if there is another liferaft nearby that can be made fast to your own.
2. Check for any leaks. Use leak stoppers and repair outfit if necessary.
3. Open Equipment Bag. Bale and dry out the raft

with baler and sponge.

4. Read canopy labels and handbook supplied.
5. Close entrances in bad or cold weather. Warmth is essential, but allow sufficient ventilation.
6. Tend the injured.
7. Check canopy light—the battery cell gives about 10 hours burning.
8. Check buoyancy chambers. If too soft, top up with bellows.
9. Set lookout watches.
10. Inflate floor with bellows if insulation from cold is needed.
11. Examine Emergency Pack, then read instructions in 'Survival Manual'.

APPENDIX

INTERNATIONAL REGULATIONS FOR
THE PREVENTION OF
COLLISIONS AT SEA
(These Regulations came into force on
1st September, 1965.)

PART A—PRELIMINARY AND DEFINITIONS

Rule 1

(*a*) These rules shall be followed by all vessels and seaplanes upon the high seas and in all waters connected therewith navigable by seagoing vessels, except as provided in Rule 30. Where, as a result of their special construction, it is not thought possible for seaplanes to comply fully with the provisions of Rules specifying the carrying of light and shapes, these provisions shall be followed as closely as circumstances permit.

(*b*) The Rules concerning lights shall be complied with in all weathers from sunset to sunrise, and during such times no other lights shall be exhibited, except such lights as cannot be mistaken for the prescribed lights or do not impair their visibility or distinctive character, or interfere with the keeping of a proper lookout. The lights prescribed by these Rules may also be exhibited from sunrise to sunset in restricted visibility and in all other circumstances when it is deemed necessary.

(*c*) In the following Rules, except where the context otherwise requires:

  (i) the word 'vessel' includes every description of water craft, other than a seaplane on the water, used or capable of being used as a means of transportation on water;

 (ii) the word 'seaplane' includes a flying boat and any other aircraft designed to manoeuvre on the water;

 (iii) the term 'power-driven vessel' means any vessel propelled by machinery;

 (iv) every power-driven vessel which is under sail and not under power is to be considered a sailing vessel, and every vessel under power, whether under sail or not, is to be considered a power-driven vessel.

  (v) a vessel or seaplane on the water is 'under way' when she is not at anchor, or made fast to the shore, or aground;

 (vi) the term 'height above the hull' means height above the uppermost continuous deck;

(vii) the length and breadth of a vessel shall be her length overall and largest breadth;

(viii) the length and span of a seaplane shall be its maximum length and span as shown in its certificate of airworthiness, or as determined by measurement in the absence of such a certificate;

(ix) vessels shall be deemed to be in sight of one another only when one can be observed visually from the other;

(x) the word 'visible', when applied to lights, means visible on a dark night with a clear atmosphere;

(xi) the term 'short blast' means a blast of about one second's duration;

(xii) the term 'prolonged blast' means a blast of from four to six seconds' duration;

(xiii) the word 'whistle' means any appliance capable of producing the prescribed short and prolonged blasts;

(xiv) the term 'engaged in fishing' means fishing with nets, liner or trawls, but does not include fishing with trolling lines.

PART B—LIGHTS AND SHAPES

Rule 2

(a) A power-driven vessel when under way shall carry:

(i) On or in front of the foremast, or if a vessel without a foremast then in the forepart of the vessel, a white light so constructed as to show an unbroken light over an arc of the horizon of 225 degrees (20 points of the compass), so fixed as to show the light $112\frac{1}{2}$ degrees (10 points) on each side of the vessel, that is from right ahead to $22\frac{1}{2}$ degrees (2 points) abaft the beam on either side, and of such a character as to be visible at a distance of at least 5 miles.

(ii) Either forward or abaft the white light prescribed in sub-section (i) a second white light similar in construction and character to that light. Vessels of less than 150 feet in length shall not be required to carry this second white light but may do so.

(iii) These two white lights shall be so placed in a line with and over the keel that one shall be at least 15 feet higher than the other and in such a position that the forward light shall always be shown lower than the after one. The horizontal distance between the two white lights shall be at least three times the vertical distance. The lower of these two white lights or, if only one is carried, then that light, shall be placed at a height above the hull of not less than 20 feet, and, if the breadth of the vessels exceeds 20 feet, then at a height above the hull not less than such breadth, so however that the height need not be placed at a greater height above the hull than 40 feet. In all circumstances the light or lights, as the case may be, shall be so placed as to be clear of and above all other lights and obstructing superstructures.

(iv) On the starboard side a green light so constructed as to show an unbroken light over an arc of the horizon of 112½ degrees (10 points of the compass), so fixed as to show the light from right ahead to 22½ degrees (2 points) abaft the beam on the starboard side, and of such a character as to be visible at a distance of at least 2 miles.

(v) On the port side a red light so constructed as to show an unbroken light over an arc of the horizon of 112½ degrees (10 points of the compass), so fixed as to show the light from right ahead to 22½ degrees (2 points) abaft the beam on the port side, and of such a character as to be visible at a distance of at least 2 miles.

(vi) The said green and red sidelights shall be fitted with inboard screens projecting at least 3 feet forward from the light, so as to prevent these lights from being seen across the bows.

(b) A seaplane under way on the water shall carry:

(i) In the forepart amidships where it can best be seen a white light, so constructed as to show an unbroken light over an arc of the horizon of 220 degrees of the compass, so fixed as to show the light 110 degrees on each side of the seaplane, namely, from right ahead to 20 degrees abaft the beam on either side, and of such a character as to be visible at a distance of at least 3 miles.

(ii) On the right or starboard wing tip a green light, so constructed as to show an unbroken light over an arc of the horizon of 110 degrees of the compass, so fixed as to show the light from right ahead to 20 degrees abaft the beam on the starboard side, and of such a character as to be visible at a distance of at least 2 miles.

(iii) On the left or port wing tip a red light, so constructed as to show an unbroken light over an arc of the horizon of 110 degrees of the compass, so fixed as to show the light from right ahead to 20 degrees abaft the beam on the port side, and of such a character as to be visible at a distance of at least 2 miles.

Rule 3

(a) A power-driven vessel when towing or pushing another vessel or seaplane shall, in addition to her sidelights, carry two white lights in a vertical line one over the other, not less than 6 feet apart, and when towing and the length of the tow, measuring from the stern of the towing vessel to the stern of the last vessel towed, exceeds 600 feet, shall carry three white lights in a vertical line one over the other, so that the upper and lower lights shall be the same distance from and not less than 6 feet above or below the middle light. Each of these lights shall be of the same construction and character and one of them shall be carried in the same position as the white light prescribed in Rule 2 (a) (i). None of these lights shall be carried at a height of less than 14 feet above the hull. In a vessel with a single mast, such lights may be carried on the mast.

(*b*) The towing vessel shall also show either the stern light prescribed in Rule 10 or in lieu of that light a small white light abaft the funnel or aftermast for the tow to steer by, but such light shall not be visible forward of the beam.

(*c*) Between sunrise and sunset a power-driven vessel engaged in towing, if the length of tow exceeds 600 feet, shall carry, where it can best be seen, a black diamond shape at least 2 feet in diameter.

(*d*) A seaplane on the water, when towing one or more seaplanes or vessels, shall carry the lights prescribed in Rule 2 (b) (i), (ii) and (iii); and, in addition, she shall carry a second white light of the same construction and character as the white light prescribed in Rule 2 (b) (i), and in a vertical line at least 6 feet above or below such light.

Rule 4

(*a*) A vessel which is not under command shall carry, where they can best be seen, and, if a power-driven vessel, in lieu of the lights prescribed in Rule 2 (a) (i) and (ii), two red lights in a vertical line one over the other not less than 6 feet apart, and of such a character as to be visible all round the horizon at a distance of at least 2 miles. By day, she shall carry in a vertical line one over the other not less than 6 feet apart, where they can best be seen, two black balls or shapes each not less than 2 feet in diameter.

(*b*) A seaplane on the water which is not under command may carry, where they can best be seen, and in lieu of the light prescribed in Rule 2 (b) (i), two red lights in a vertical line, one over the other, not less than 3 feet apart, and of such a character as to be visible all round the horizon at a distance of at least 2 miles, and may by day carry in a vertical line one over the other not less than 3 feet apart, where they can best be seen, two black balls or shapes, each not less than 2 feet in diameter.

(*c*) A vessel engaged in laying or in picking up a submarine cable or navigation mark, or a vessel engaged in surveying or underwater operations, or a vessel engaged in replenishment at sea, or in the launching or recovery of aircraft when from the nature of her work she is unable to get out of the way of approaching vessels, shall carry, in lieu of the lights prescribed in Rule 2 (a) (i) and (ii), or Rule 7 (a) (i), three lights in a vertical line one over the other so that the upper and lower lights shall be the same distance from, and not less than 6 feet above or below, the middle light. The highest and lowest of these lights shall be red, and the middle light shall be white, and they shall be of such a character as to be visible all round the horizon at a distance of at least 2 miles. By day, she shall carry in a vertical line one over the other not less than 6 feet apart, where they can best be seen, three shapes each not less than 2 feet in diameter, of which the highest and lowest shall be globular in shape and red in colour, and the middle one diamond in shape and white.

(*d*) (i) A vessel engaged in minesweeping operations shall carry at the fore truck a green light, and at the end or ends of the fore yard on the side or sides on which danger exists, another such light or lights. These lights shall be carried in addition to the light prescribed in Rule 2 (a) (i) or Rule 7 (a) (i), as appropriate, and shall be of such a character as to be visible all round the horizon at a distance of at least 2 miles. By day, she shall carry black balls, not less than 2 feet in diameter, in the same position as the green lights.

(ii) The showing of these lights or balls indicates that it is dangerous for other vessels to approach closer than 3000 feet astern of the minesweeper or 1500 feet on the other side or sides on which danger exists.

(*e*) The vessels and seaplanes referred to in this Rule, when not making way through the water, shall show neither the coloured sidelights nor the stern light, but when making way they shall show them.

(*f*) The lights and shapes prescribed in this Rule are to be taken by other vessels and seaplanes as signals that the vessel or seaplane showing them is not under command and cannot therefore get out of the way.

(*g*) These signals are not signals of vessels in distress and requiring assistance. Such signals are contained in Rule 31.

Rule 5

(*a*) A sailing vessel under way and any vessel or seaplane being towed shall carry the same lights as are prescribed in Rule 2 for a power-driven vessel or a seaplane under way, respectively, with the exception of the white lights prescribed therein, which they shall never carry. They shall also carry stern lights as prescribed in Rule 10, provided that vessel towed, except the last vessel of a tow, may carry, in lieu of such stern light, a small white light as prescribed in Rule 3 (b).

(*b*) In addition to the lights prescribed in section (a), a sailing vessel may carry on the top of a foremast two lights in a vertical line one over the other, sufficiently separated so as to be clearly distinguished. The upper light shall be red and the lower light shall be green. Both lights shall be constructed and fixed as prescribed in Rule 2 (a) (i) and shall be visible at a distance of at least 2 miles.

(c) A vessel being pushed ahead shall carry, at the forward end, on the starboard side a green light and on the port side a red light, which shall have the same characteristics as the lights prescribed in Rule 2 (a) (iv) and (v) and shall be screened as provided in Rule 2 (a) (vi), provided that any number of vessels pushed ahead in a group shall be lighted as one vessel.

(d) Between sunrise and sunset a vessel being towed, if the length of the two exceeds 600 feet, shall carry where it can best be seen a black diamond shape at least 2 feet in diameter.

Rule 6

(a) When it is not possible on account of bad weather or other sufficient cause to fix the green and red sidelights, these lights shall be kept at hand lighted and ready for immediate use, and shall, on the approach of or to other vessels, be exhibited on their respective sides in sufficient time to prevent collision, in such manner as to make them most visible, and so that the green light shall not be seen on the port side nor the red light on the starboard side, not, if practicable, more than $22\frac{1}{2}$ degrees (2 points) abaft the beam on their respective sides.

(b) To make use of these portable lights more certain and easy, the lanterns containing them shall each be painted outside with the colour of the lights they respectively contain, and shall be provided with proper screens.

Rule 7

Power-driven vessels of less than 85 feet in length, vessels under oars or sails of less than 40 feet in length, and rowing boats, when under way, shall not be required to carry the lights prescribed in Rules 2, 3 and 5, but if they do not carry them they shall be provided with the following lights:

(a) Power-driven vessels of less than 65 feet in length, except as provided in sections (b) and (c), shall carry:

(i) In the forepart of the vessel, where it can best be seen, and at a height above the gunwale or not less than 9 feet, a white light constructed and fixed as prescribed in Rule 2 (a) (i) and of such a character as to be visible at a distance of at least 3 miles.

(ii) Green and red sidelights constructed and fixed as prescribed in Rule 2 (a) (iv) and (v), and of such a character as to be visible at a distance of at least 1 mile, or a combined lantern showing a green light and a red light from right ahead to $22\frac{1}{2}$ degrees (2 points) abaft the beam on their respective sides. Such lanterns shall be carried not less than 3 feet below the white light.

(*b*) Power-driven vessels of less than 65 feet in length when towing or pushing another vessel shall carry:

  (i) In addition to the sidelights or the combined lantern prescribed in section (a) (ii) two white lights in a vertical line, one over the other not less than 4 feet apart. Each of these lights shall be of the same construction and character as the white light prescribed in section (a) (i) and one of them shall be carried in the same position. In a vessel with a single mast such lights may be carried on the mast.

  (ii) Either a stern light as prescribed in Rule 10 or in lieu of that light a small white light abaft the funnel or aftermast for the tow to steer by, but such light shall not be visible forward of the beam.

(*c*) Power-driven vessels of less than 40 feet in length may carry the white light at a height less than 9 feet above the gunwale but it shall be carried not less than 3 feet above the sidelights or the combined lantern prescribed in section (a) (ii).

(*d*) Vessels of less than 40 feet in length, under oars or sails, except as provided in section (f), shall, if they do not carry the sidelights, carry, where it can best be seen, a lantern showing a green light on one side and a red light on the other, of such a character as to be visible at a distance of at least 1 mile, and so fixed that the green light shall not be seen on the port side, nor the red light on the starboard side. Where it is not possible to fix this light, it shall be kept ready for immediate use and shall be exhibited in sufficient time to prevent collision and so that the green light shall not be seen on the port side nor the red light on the starboard side.

(*e*) The vessels referred to in this Rule when being towed shall carry the sidelights or the combined lantern prescribed in sections (a) or (d) of this Rule, as appropriate, and a stern light as prescribed in Rule 10, or, except the last vessel of the tow, a small white light as prescribed in section (b) (ii). When being pushed ahead they shall carry at the forward end the sidelights or combined lantern prescribed in sections (a) or (d) of this Rule, as appropriate, provided that any number of vessels referred to in this Rule when pushed ahead in a group shall be lighted as one vessel under this Rule unless the overall length of the group exceeds 65 feet when the provisions of Rule 5 (c) shall apply.

(*f*) Small rowing boats, whether under oars or sail, shall only be required to have ready at hand an electric torch or a lighted lantern, showing a white light, which shall be exhibited in sufficient time to prevent collision.

(*g*) The vessels and boats referred to in this Rule shall not be required to carry the lights or shapes prescribed in Rules 4 (a) and 11 (e) and the size of their day signals may be less than is prescribed in Rules 4 (c) and 11 (c).

Rule 8

(*a*) A power-driven pilot-vessel when engaged on pilotage duty and under way:

  (i) Shall carry a white light at the masthead at a height of not less than 20 feet above the hull, visible all round the horizon at a distance of at least 3 miles, and at a distance of 8 feet below it a red light similar in construction and character. If such a vessel is of less than 65 feet she may carry the white light at a height of not less than 9 feet above the gunwale and the red light at a distance of 4 feet below the white light.

 (ii) Shall carry the sidelights or lanterns prescribed in Rule 2 (a) (iv) and (v) or Rule 7 (a) (ii) or (d), as appropriate, and the stern light prescribed in Rule 10.

(iii) Shall show one or more flare-up lights at intervals not exceeding 10 minutes. An intermittent white light visible all round the horizon may be used in lieu of flare-up lights.

(*b*) A sailing pilot-vessel when engaged on pilotage duty and under way:

  (i) Shall carry a white light at the masthead visible all round the horizon at a distance of at least 3 miles.

 (ii) Shall be provided with the sidelights or lantern prescribed in Rules 5 (a) or 7 (d), as appropriate, and shall, on the near approach of or to other vessels, have such lights ready for use, and shall show them at short intervals to indicate the direction in which she is heading, but the green light shall not be shown on the port side nor the red light on the starboard side. She shall also carry the stern light prescribed in Rule 10.

(iii) Shall show one or more flare-up lights at intervals not exceeding 10 minutes.

(*c*) A pilot-vessel when engaged on pilotage duty and not under way shall carry the lights and show the flares prescribed in sections (a) (i) and (iii) or (b) (i) and (iii), as appropriate, and if at anchor shall also carry the anchor lights prescribed in Rule 11.

(*d*) A pilot-vessel when not engaged on pilotage duty shall show the lights or shapes for a similar vessel of her length.

Rule 9

(*a*) Fishing vessels when not engaged in fishing shall show the lights or shapes for similar vessels of their length.

(*b*) Vessels engaged in fishing, when under way or at anchor, shall show only the lights and shapes prescribed in this Rule, which lights and shapes shall be visible at a distance of at least 2 miles.

(*c*) (i) Vessels when engaged in trawling, by which is meant the dragging of a dredge net or other apparatus through the water, shall carry two lights in a vertical line, one over the other, not less than 4 feet nor more than 12 feet apart. The upper of these lights shall be green and the lower light white, and each shall be visible all round the horizon. The lower of these two lights shall be carried at a height above the sidelights not less than twice the distance between the two vertical lights.

(ii) Such vessels may in addition carry a white light similar in construction to the white light prescribed in Rule 2 (a) (i) but such light shall be carried lower than and abaft the all-round green and white lights.

(*d*) Vessels when engaged in fishing, except vessels engaged in trawling, shall carry the lights prescribed in section (c) (i) except that the upper of the two vertical lights shall be red. Such vessels if of less than 40 feet in length may carry the red light at a height of not less than 9 feet above the gunwale and the white light not less than 3 feet below the red light.

(*e*) Vessels referred to in sections (c) and (d), when making way through the water, shall carry the sidelights or lanterns prescribed in Rule 2 (a) (iv) and (v) or Rule 7 (a) (ii) or (d), as appropriate, and the stern light prescribed in Rule 10. When not making way through the water they shall show neither the sidelights nor the stern light.

(*f*) Vessels referred to in section (d) with outlying gear extending more than 500 feet horizontally into the seaway shall carry an additional all-round white light at a horizontal distance of not less than 6 feet nor more than 20 feet away from the vertical lights in the direction of the outlying gear. This additional white light shall be placed at a height not exceeding that of the white light prescribed in section (c) (i) and not lower than sidelights.

(*g*) In addition to the lights which they are required by this Rule to carry, vessels engaged in fishing may, if necessary, in order to attract the attention of an approaching vessel, use a flare-up light, or may direct the beam of their searchlight in the direction of a danger threatening the approaching vessel, in such a way as not to embarrass other vessels. They may also use working lights, but fishermen shall take into account that specially bright or insufficiently screened working lights may impair the visibility and distinctive character of the lights prescribed in this Rule.

(*h*) By day vessels when engaged in fishing shall indicate their occupation by displaying where it can best be seen a black shape consisting of two cones each not less than 2 feet diameter with their points together one above the other. Such vessels if of less than 65 feet in length may substitute a basket for such black shape. If their outlying gear extends more than 500 feet horizontally into the seaway vessels engaged in fishing shall display in addition one black conical shape, point upwards, in the direction of the outlying gear.

Rule 10

(*a*) Except where otherwise provided in these Rules, a vessel when under way shall carry at her stern a white light so constructed that it shall show an unbroken light over an arc of the horizon of 135 degrees (12 points of the compass), so fixed as to show the light $67\frac{1}{2}$ degrees (6 points) from right aft on each side of the vessel, and of such a character as to be visible at a distance of at least 2 miles.

(*b*) In a small vessel, if it is not possible on account of bad weather or other sufficient cause for this light to be fixed, an electric torch or a lighted lantern showing a white light shall be kept at hand ready for use and shall, on the approach of an overtaking vessel, be shown in sufficient time to prevent collision.

(*c*) A seaplane on the water when under way shall carry on her tail a white light, so constructed as to show an unbroken light over an arc of the horizon of 140 degrees of the compass, so fixed as to show the light 70 degrees from right aft on each side of the seaplane, and of such a character as to be visible at a distance of at least 2 miles.

Rule 11

(*a*) A vessel of less than 150 feet in length, when at anchor, shall carry in the forepart of the vessel, where it can best be seen, a white light visible all round the horizon at a distance of at least 2 miles. Such a vessel may also carry a second white light in the position prescribed in section (b) of this Rule but shall not be required to do so. The second white light, if carried, shall be visible at a distance of at least 2 miles and so placed as to be as far as possible visible all round the horizon.

(*b*) A vessel of 150 feet or more in length, when at anchor, shall carry near the stern of the vessel, at a height of not less than 20 feet above the hull, one such light, and at or near the stern of the vessel and at such a height that it shall be not less than 15 feet lower than the forward light, another such light. Both these lights shall be visible at a distance of at least 3 miles and so placed as to be as far as possible visible all round the horizon.

(*c*) Between sunrise and sunset every vessel when at anchor shall carry in the forepart of the vessel, where it can best be seen, one black ball not less than 2 feet in diameter.

(*d*) A vessel engaged in laying or in picking up a submarine cable or navigation mark, or a vessel engaged in surveying or underwater operations, when at anchor, shall carry the lights or shapes prescribed in Rule 4 (c) in addition to those prescribed in the appropriate preceding sections of this Rule.

(*e*) A vessel aground shall carry the light or lights prescribed in sections (a) or (b) and the two red lights prescribed in Rule 4 (a). By day she shall carry, where they can best be seen, three black balls, each not less than 2 feet in diameter, placed in a vertical line one over the other, not less than 6 feet apart.

(*f*) A seaplane on the water under 150 feet in length, when at anchor, shall carry, where it can best be seen, a white light, visible all round the horizon at a distance of at least 2 miles.

(*g*) A seaplane on the water 150 feet or upwards in length, when at anchor, shall carry, where they can best be seen, a white light forward and a white light aft, both lights visible all round the horizon at a distance of at least 3 miles; and, in addition, if the seaplane is more than 150 feet in span, a white light on each side to indicate the maximum span, and visible, so far as practicable, all round the horizon at a distance of 1 mile.

(*h*) A seaplane aground shall carry an anchor light or lights as prescribed in sections (f) and (g), and in addition may carry two red lights in a vertical line, at least 3 feet apart, so placed as to be visible all round the horizon.

Rule 12

Every vessel or seaplane on the water may, if necessary in order to attract attention, in addition to the lights which she is by these Rules required to carry, show a flare-up light or use a detonating or other efficient sound signal that cannot be mistaken for any signal authorised elsewhere under these Rules.

Rule 13

(*a*) Nothing in these Rules shall interfere with the operations of any special rules made by the Government of any nation with respect to additional station and signal lights for ships of war, for vessels sailing under convoy, for fishing vessels engaged in fishing as a fleet or for seaplanes on the water.

(*b*) Whenever the Government concerned shall have determined that a naval or other military vessel or waterborne seaplane of special construction or purpose cannot comply fully with the provisions of any of these Rules with respect to the number, position, range or arc of visibility of lights or shapes, without interfering with the military function of the vessel or seaplane, such vessel or seaplane shall comply with such other provisions in regard to the number, position, range or arc of visibility of lights or shapes as her Government shall have determined to be the closest possible compliance with these Rules in respect of that vessel or seaplane.

Rule 14

A vessel proceeding under sail, when also being propelled by machinery, shall carry in the daytime forward, where it can best be seen, one black conical shape, point downwards, not less than 2 feet in diameter at its base.

PART C—SOUND SIGNALS AND CONDUCT IN RESTRICTED VISIBILITY

Preliminary

1. *The possession of information obtained from radar does not relieve any vessel of the obligation of conforming strictly with the rules and, in particular, the obligations contained in Rules 15 and 16.*

2. *The Annex to the Rules contains recommendations intended to assist in the use of radar as an aid to avoiding collision in restricted visibility.*

Rule 15

(*a*) A power-driven vessel of 40 feet or more in length shall be provided with an efficient whistle, sounded by steam or by some substitute for steam, so placed that the sound may not be intercepted by any obstruction, and with an efficient fog horn to be sounded by mechanical means, and also with an efficient bell. A sailing vessel of 40 feet or more in length shall be provided with a similar fog horn and bell.

(*b*) All signals prescribed in this Rule for vessels under way shall be given:

    (i)   by power-driven vessels on the whistle;

    (ii) by sailing vessels on the fog horn;

    (iii) by vessels towed on the whistle or fog horn.

(*c*) In fog, mist, falling snow, heavy rainstorms, or any other condition similarly restricting visibility, whether by day or night, the signals prescribed in this Rule shall be used as follows:

    (i)   A power-driven vessel making way through the water shall sound at intervals of not more than 2 minutes a prolonged blast.

    (ii) A power-driven vessel under way, but stopped and making no way through the water, shall sound at intervals of not more than two minutes two prolonged blasts, with an interval of about 1 second between them.

    (iii) A sailing vessel under way shall sound, at intervals of not more than 1 minute, when on the starboard tack one blast, when on the port tack two blasts in succession, and when with the wind abaft the beam three blasts in succession.

    (iv) A vessel when at anchor shall at intervals of not more than 1 minute ring the bell rapidly for about 5 seconds. In vessels of more than 350 feet in length the bell shall be sounded in the forepart of the vessel and, in addition, there shall be sounded in the after part of the vessel, at intervals of not more than 1 minute for about 5 seconds, a gong or other instrument, the tone and sounding of which cannot be confused with that of the bell. Every vessel at anchor may in addition, in accordance with Rule 12, sound three blasts in succession, namely, one short, one prolonged and one short blast, to give warning of her position and of the possibility of collision to an approaching vessel.

(v) A vessel when towing, a vessel engaged in laying or in picking up a submarine cable or navigation mark, and a vessel under way which is unable to get out of the way of an approaching vessel through not being under command or unable to manoeuvre as required by these Rules shall, instead of the signals prescribed in sub-sections (i), (ii) and (iii), sound, at intervals of not more than 1 minute, three blasts in succession, namely, one prolonged blast followed by two short blasts.

(vi) A vessel towed, or, if more than one vessel is towed, only the last vessel of the tow, if manned, shall, at intervals of not more than 1 minute, sound four blasts in succession, namely, one prolonged blast followed by three short blasts. When practicable, this signal shall be made immediately after the signal made by the towing vessel.

(vii) A vessel aground shall give the bell signal and, if required, the gong signal, prescribed in sub-section (iv), and shall, in addition, give three separate and distinct strokes on the bell immediately before and after such rapid ringing of the bell.

(viii) A vessel engaged in fishing when under way or at anchor shall at intervals of not more than 1 minute sound the signal prescribed in sub-section (v). A vessel when fishing with trolling lines and under way shall sound the signals prescribed in sub-sections (i), (ii) or (iii) as may be appropriate.

(ix) A vessel of less than 40 feet in length, a rowing boat, or a seaplane on the water, shall not be obliged to give the above-mentioned signals but if she does not, she shall make some other efficient sound signals at intervals of not more than 1 minute.

(x) A power-driven pilot-vessel when engaged in pilotage duty may, in addition to the signals prescribed in sub-sections (i), (ii) and (iv), sound an identity signal consisting of four short blasts.

Rule 16

(a) Every vessel, or seaplane when taxi-ing on the water, shall, in fog, mist, falling snow, heavy rainstorms or any other condition similarly restricting visibility, go at a moderate speed, having careful regard to the existing circumstances and conditions.

(*b*) A power-driven vessel hearing, apparently forward of her beam, the fog signal of a vessel the position of which is not ascertained, shall, so far as the circumstances of the case admit, stop her engines, and then navigate with caution until danger of collision is over.

(*c*) A power-driven vessel which detects the presence of another vessel forward of her beam before hearing her fog signal or sighting her visually may take early and substantial action to avoid a close quarters situation but, if this cannot be avoided, she shall, so far as the circumstances of the case admit, stop her engines in proper time to avoid a collision and then navigate with caution until danger of collision is over.

PART D—STEERING AND SAILING RULES

Preliminary

1. In obeying and construing these Rules, any action taken should be positive, in ample time, and with due regard to the observance of good seamanship.

2. Risk of collision can, when circumstances permit, be ascertained by carefully watching the compass bearing of an approaching vessel. If the bearing does not appreciably change, such risk should be deemed to exist.

3. Mariners should bear in mind that seaplanes in the act of landing or taking off, or operating under adverse weather conditions, may be unable to change their intended action at the last moment.

4. Rules 17 to 24 apply only to vessels in sight of one another.

Rule 17

(*a*) When two sailing vessels are approaching one another, so as to involve risk of collision, one of them shall keep out of the way of the other as follows:

  (i) When each has the wind on a different side, the vessel which has the wind on the port side shall keep out of the way of the other.

 (ii) When both have the wind on the same side, the vessel which is to windward shall keep out of the way of the vessel which is to leeward.

(*b*) For the purposes of this Rule the windward side shall be deemed to be the side opposite to that on which the mainsail is carried or, in the case of a square-rigged vessel, the side opposite to that on which the largest fore-and-aft sail is carried.

Rule 18

(*a*) When two power-driven vessels are meeting end on, or nearly end on, so as to involve risk of collision, each shall alter her course to starboard so that each may pass on the port side of the other. This Rule only applies to cases where vessels are meeting end on, or nearly end on, in such manner as to involve risk of collision, and does not apply to two vessels which must, if both keep on their respective courses, pass clear of each other. The only cases to which it does apply are when each of two vessels is end on, or nearly end on, to the other; in other words, to cases in which, by day, each vessel sees the masts of the other in a line, or nearly in a line, with her own; and by night, to cases in which each vessel is in such a position as to see both the sidelights of the other. It does not apply, by day, to cases in which a vessel sees another ahead crossing her own course; or, by night, to cases where the red light of one vessel is opposed to the red light of the other, or where the green light of one vessel is opposed to the green light of the other, or where a red light without a green light or a green light without a red light is seen ahead, or where both green and red lights are seen anywhere but ahead.

(*b*) For the purposes of this Rule and Rules 19 to 29 inclusive, except Rule 20 (c) and Rule 28, a seaplane on the water shall be deemed to be a vessel, and the expression 'power-driven vessel' shall be construed accordingly.

Rule 19

When two power-driven vessels are crossing, so as to involve risk of collision, the vessel which has the other on her own starboard side shall keep out of the way of the other.

Rule 20

(*a*) When a power-driven vessel and a sailing vessel are proceeding in such directions as to involve risk of collision, except as provided for in Rules 24 and 26, the power-driven vessel shall keep out of the way of the sailing vessel.

(*b*) This Rule shall not give to a sailing vessel the right to hamper, in a narrow channel, the safe passage of a power-driven vessel which can navigate only inside such channel.

(*c*) A seaplane on the water shall, in general, keep well clear of all vessels and avoid impeding their navigation. In circumstances, however, where risk of collision exists, she shall comply with these Rules.

Rule 21

Where by any of these Rules one of two vessels is to keep out of the way, the other shall keep her course and speed. When, from any cause, the latter vessel finds herself so close that collision cannot be avoided by the action of the giving-way vessel alone, she also shall take such action as will best aid to avert collision (see Rules 27 and 29).

Rule 22

Every vessel which is directed by these Rules to keep out of the way of another vessel shall, so far as possible, take positive early action to comply with this obligation, and shall, if the circumstances of the case admit, avoid crossing ahead of the other.

Rule 23

Every power-driven vessel which is directed by these Rules to keep out of the way of another vessel shall, on approaching her, if necessary, slacken her speed or stop or reverse.

Rule 24

(a) Notwithstanding anything contained in these Rules, every vessel overtaking any other shall keep out of the way of the overtaken vessel.

(b) Every vessel coming up with another vessel from any direction more than $22\frac{1}{2}$ degrees (2 points) abaft her beam, i.e. in such a position, with reference to the vessel which she is overtaking, that at night she would be unable to see either of that vessel's sidelights, shall be deemed to be an overtaking vessel; and no subsequent alteration of the bearing between the two vessels shall make the overtaking vessel a crossing vessel within the meaning of these Rules, or relieve her of the duty of keeping clear of the overtaken vessel until she is finally past and clear.

(c) If the overtaken vessel cannot determine with certainty whether she is forward of or abaft this direction from the other vessel, she shall assume that she is an overtaking vessel and keep out of the way.

Rule 25

(a) In a narrow channel every power-driven vessel when proceeding along the course of the channel shall, when it is safe, and practicable, keep to that side of the fairway or mid-channel which lies on the starboard side of such vessel.

(b) Whenever a power-driven vessel is nearing a bend a channel where a vessel approaching from the other direction cannot be seen, such power-driven vessel, when she shall have arrived within one-half ($\frac{1}{2}$) mile of the bend, shall give a signal by one prolonged blast on her whistle, which signal shall be answered by a similar blast by any approaching power-driven vessel that may be within hearing around the bend. Regardless of whether an approaching vessel on the farther side of the bend is heard, such bend shall be rounded with alertness and caution.

(c) In a narrow channel a power-driven vessel of less than 65 feet in length shall not hamper the safe passage of a vessel which can navigate only inside such channel.

Rule 26

All vessels not engaged in fishing, except vessels to which the provisions of Rule 4 apply, shall, when under way, keep out of the way of vessels engaged in fishing. This Rule shall not give to any vessel engaged in fishing the right of obstructing a fairway used by vessels other than fishing vessels.

Rule 27

In obeying and construing these Rules due regard shall be had to all dangers of navigation and collision, and to any special circumstances, including the limitations of the craft involved, which may render a departure from the above Rules necessary in order to avoid immediate danger.

PART E—SOUND SIGNALS FOR VESSELS IN SIGHT OF ONE ANOTHER

Rule 28

(*a*) When vessels are in sight of one another, a power-driven vessel under way, in taking any course authorised or required by these Rules, shall indicate that course by the following signals on her whistle, namely:

One short blast to mean
'I am altering my course to starboard'.
Two short blasts to mean
'I am altering my course to port'.
Three short blasts to mean
'My engines are going astern'.

(*b*) Whenever a power-driven vessel which, under these Rules, is to keep her course and speed, is in sight of another vessel and is in doubt whether sufficient action is being taken by the other vessel to avert collision, she may indicate such doubt by giving at least five short and rapid blasts on the whistle. The giving of such a signal shall not relieve a vessel of her obligations under Rules 27 and 29 or any other Rule, or of her duty to indicate any action taken under these Rules by giving the appropriate sound signals laid down in this Rule.

(*c*) Any whistle signal mentioned in this Rule may be further indicated by a visual signal consisting of a white light visible all round the horizon at a distance of at least 5 miles, and so devised that it will operate simultaneously and in conjunction with the whistle-sounding mechanism and remain lighted and visible during the same period as the sound signal.

(*d*) Nothing in these Rules shall interfere with the operation of any special rules made by the Government of any nation with respects to the use of additional whistle signals between ships of war or vessels sailing under convoy.

PART F—MISCELLANEOUS

Rule 29

Nothing in these Rules shall exonerate any vessel, or the owner, master or crew thereof, from the consequences of any neglect to carry lights or signals, or of any neglect to keep a proper lookout, or of the neglect of any precaution which may be required by the ordinary practice of seamen, or by the special circumstances of the case.

Rule 30

Nothing in these Rules shall interfere with the operation of a special rule duly made by local authority relative to the navigation of any harbour, river, lake, or inland water, including a reserved seaplane area.

Rule 31
Distress Signals

(a) When a vessel or seaplane on the water is in distress and requires assistance from other vessels or from the shore, the following shall be the signals to be used or displayed by her, either together or separately, namely:

   (i) A gun or other explosive signal fired at intervals of about a minute.
  (ii) A continuous sounding with any fog signalling apparatus.
 (iii) Rockets or shells, throwing red stars fired one at a time at short intervals.
  (iv) A signal made by radiotelegraphy or by any other signalling method consisting of the group · · · – – – · · · in the Morse Code.
   (v) A signal sent by radiotelephony consisting of the spoken word 'Mayday'.
  (vi) The International Code Signal of distress indicated by N.C.
 (vii) A signal consisting of a square flag having above or below it a ball or anything resembling a ball.
(viii) Flames on the vessel (as from a burning tar barrel, oil barrel, etc.).
  (ix) A rocket parachute flare or a hand flare showing a red light.
   (x) A smoke signal giving off a volume of orange-coloured smoke.
  (xi) Slowly and repeatedly raising and lowering arms outstretched to each side.

Note: Vessels in distress may use the radiotelegraph alarm signal or the radiotelephone alarm signal to secure attention to distress calls and messages. The radiotelegraph alarm signal, which is designed to actuate the radiotelegraph auto alarms of vessels so fitted, consists of a series of twelve dashes, sent in 1 minute, the duration of each dash being 4 seconds, and the duration of the interval between two consecutive dashes being 1 second. The radiotelephone alarm signal consists of two tones transmitted alternatively over periods of from 30 seconds to 1 minute.

(*b*) The use of any of the foregoing signals, except for the purpose of indicating that a vessel or seaplane is in distress, and the use of any signals which may be confused with any of the above signals, is prohibited.

ANNEX TO THE RULES
RECOMMENDATIONS ON THE USE OF RADAR INFORMATION AS AN AID TO AVOIDING COLLISIONS AT SEA

(1) Assumptions made on scanty information may be dangerous and should be avoided.

(2) A vessel navigating with the aid of radar in restricted visibility must, in compliance with Rules 16 (a), go at a moderate speed. Information obtained from the use of radar is one of the circumstances to be taken into account when determining moderate speed. In this regard it must be recognised that small vessels, small icebergs and similar floating objects may not be detected by radar. Radar indications of one or more vessels in the vicinity may mean that 'moderate speed' should be slower than a mariner without radar might consider moderate in the circumstances.

(3) When navigating in restricted visibility the radar range and bearing alone do not constitute ascertainment of the position of the other vessel under Rule 16 (b) sufficiently to relieve a vessel of the duty to stop her engines and navigate with caution when a fog signal is heard forward of the beam.

(4) When action has been taken under Rule 16 (c) to avoid a close quarters situation, it is essential to make sure that such action is having the desired effect. Alterations of course or speed or both are matters as to which the mariner must be guided by the circumstances of the case.

(5) Alteration of course alone may be the most effective action to avoid close quarters provided that:

(a) There is sufficient sea room.
(b) It is made in good time.
(c) It is substantial. A succession of small alterations of course should be avoided.
(d) It does not result in a close quarters situation with other vessels.

(6) The direction of an alteration of course is a matter in which the mariner must be guided by the circumstances of the case. An alteration to starboard, particularly when vessels are approaching apparently on opposite or nearly opposite courses, is generally preferable to an alteration to port.

(7) An alteration of speed, either alone or in conjunction with an alteration of course, should be substantial. A number of small alterations of speed should be avoided.

(8) If a close quarters situation is imminent, the most prudent action may be to take all way off the vessel.

CONVERSION TABLES

ENGLISH MEASURES TO METRIC MEASURES

Pounds...	to kilos...	×	0·45357
Hundredweights (cwt)	to kilos...	×	50·80
Tons	to kilos...	×	1016·00
Lineal inches	to millimetres	×	25·3999
Lineal feet	to millimetres	×	304·7997
Lineal yards	to millimetres	×	914·3992
Lineal fathoms... ...	to millimetres	×	1828·7984
Lineal inches	to metres	×	0·0254
Lineal feet	to metres	×	0·3048
Lineal yards	to metres	×	0·9144
Lineal fathoms... ...	to metres	×	1·8288
Pounds per lineal foot	to kilos per metre	×	1·4881
Pounds per lineal yard...	to kilos per metre	×	0·4960
Pounds per lineal fathom	to kilos per metre	×	0·2480
Tons per square inch	to kilos per square millimetre	×	1·5748
Square inch	to square millimetre	×	645·1549

METRIC MEASURES TO ENGLISH MEASURES

Kilos	to pounds	×	2·204724
Kilos	to cwts	×	0·019685
Kilos	to tons	×	0·000984
Millimetres	to inches	×	0·039370
Millimetres	to feet	×	0·003281
Millimetres	to yards	×	0·001094
Millimetres	to fathoms	×	0·000547
Metres	to inches	×	39·370113
Metres	to feet	×	3·280842
Metres	to yards	×	1·093614
Metres	to fathoms	×	0·546807
Kilos per lineal metre	to pounds per Foot...	×	0·671999
Kilos per lineal metre	to pounds per Yard	×	2·015998
Kilos per lineal metre	to pounds per Fathom	×	4·031997
Kilos per square millimetre	to tons per square inch	×	0·634997
Square millimetre ...	to square inch	×	0·001550

To convert diameter into circumference, multiply by 3·14159.
To convert circumference into diameter, multiply by 0·3183.
One-eighth of an inch of circumference = one mm of diameter.
Mm of Diameter ÷ 8 = circumference in inches.